ILLUSTRATION NEXT

ANA BENAROYA

ILLUSTRATION NEXT

CONTEMPORARY
CREATIVE
COLLABORATION

382 illustrations, 334 in color

Thames & Hudson

CONTENTS

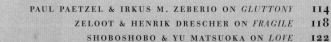

OPPOSITE: Paul Loubet, "Gregol et
Poluar, Champion du Ping Pong,"
personal work, ink on paper, digital
color, 2009
OVERLEAF: Mu Pan, "China Book,"
chapter 4, watercolor, 2009

Introduction

In the past decade illustration has undergone an amazing renaissance. Not only have illustrators continued to work in traditional printed venues, but with the proliferation of the internet and social media, the venues in which illustrators can work have grown multifold. Additionally, the widespread influence of illustration on popular culture and the general populace has increased significantly. The accessibility of this kind of imagery to the non-artist is paramount in explaining why illustration has become valued both commercially and critically.

Often falling in the shadow of the fine art world, illustration has many times been cast aside as mere decoration and the work of hired hands, while illustrators have been seen as craftsmen rather than true artists with higher goals in mind. But the reality of today's fine art world is that it has increasingly become an exclusive playground for the extremely wealthy and, as a result, art has seemingly lost its purpose in modern society. This is a loss both for the world and for art. The majority of the population is not educated about art history and never comes into contact with working artists or their artwork.

However, with the rise of illustration, this seems to be changing. The illustrator was previously a solitary figure, working alone and "for hire," but the internet has brought this community together. Illustrators can now instantly view each other's work, collaborate, and share ideas as never before. It is the illustrators who are in touch with the current modes of thought and modern trends that shape the world in which we live. They develop and shape the visual language that the non-artist comes into contact with almost everyday of their life. They communicate with and on behalf of the rest of the world, literally and emotionally. It is because of this relevance that

I believe illustration is the most interesting and important section of the art world today.

When I first came up with the concept for this project I knew I wanted to create a book that framed illustration in this light. I wanted to look at illustrators working today who I believe are at the forefront of this renaissance – those who understand that illustration has a power both to communicate and to become a higher form of personal expression. I intentionally approached these 50 illustrators as one would traditionally approach a fine artist. The questions I asked were aimed at getting them to talk about who they are as people, what their philosophies are, not simply about their technique and their clients. How they approach these questions is telling in itself.

This book is essentially divided into segments of two kinds. One features the illustrator as a solo artist, including a brief interview and samples of both their commercial and personal work; and the second part pairs each artist with another, and shows their collaboration on an open-ended assigned theme. The work created for the collaboration is completely original and has never been seen or published before.

With the collaborations, I decided to give the artists an open-ended, one-word topic, along with instructions that they should work together and fill four pages. When choosing the themes for these briefs I knew I wanted to choose words that were completely vague and deeply philosophical at the same time. I wanted to allow these words to resonate with the artists and allow them to transform this "assignment" into something wholly self-guided and personal.

I chose which briefs to give to which pair of illustrators by instinct. I tried to look at both their bodies of work and select something that I felt was already in their visual language.

'There seemed to be several ways the pairs approached the collaboration. Some simply divided the pages in half and each artist approached the theme as they wished on their own.'

Of course, I had no way of predicting how they would see the word I had chosen or what sort of implications it might have for them both visually and emotionally. There seemed to be several ways the pairs approached the collaboration. Some simply divided the pages in half and each artist approached the theme as they wished on their own. With this approach there were, inevitably, various levels of discussion between the artists before each went off on their own way. Mu Pan and Ryan Cecil Smith approached the collaboration in this way, with minimal discussion beforehand. Other artists divided the pages, yet worked together in a kind of creative dialogue, for instance, Whitney Sherman and Josephin Ritschel on their theme of EXCESS. The images were made by each artist, but the way the theme is presented relates heavily to the other's work. In this way, the collaboration was very much conceptual and thematic, rather than sharing the same physical space.

Other artists, such as Café con Leche and Brecht Vandenbroucke, divided the pages, yet worked together on their theme of DEATH to make a work over a two-page spread. They chose to have one spread where their two pages connected to make one image and to have two separate images on the other spread, each one the personal vision of the artist.

And finally, other artists chose to work together on each page. Some, such as Gustavo Eandi and Simon Roussin, divided the page into sections and each artist had certain assigned sections. The finished result ended up becoming comic-like. While others, such as myself and Mike Perry, chose to work directly on top of each other's drawing, in the end producing one image using both our hands.

In a sense, these collaborations forced the illustrators to become the ones in charge of the interview; they had to ask the questions of each other and themselves. Working with each other forced the illustrators to come face to face with their own notions of not only the subject matter, but also the very way they saw themselves as artists. They now had to consider what their idea of artistic individuality was, why they approach image-making in the way they do, and how best to communicate both with each other and the future viewers of the work.

With these collaborations I sought not only to bring out the individual voices of these illustrators, but also to emphasize the idea of art as a communicator and a connector of people. This is the reason I think illustration has undergone a renaissance in recent years. We live in a world that seems to place more and more importance on speed, technology, and new-ness. We are bombarded everyday with so much information and imagery that we begin to forget who we are as people, as humans. Amidst all this noise and chaos, deep down we all desire the same things: to connect with other humans, to love, and to be loved. Illustration provides this humanity. The fact that it is hand-drawn humanizes whatever it is we may be looking at in the moment, be it a page from a magazine, a T-shirt, or an article on a website.

While there have been many compendiums of work made about illustrators, both in print and online, no book exists that provides insights into what inspires and motivates the illustrators in their art. No book has yet tried to knock down the brick wall that often stands between the fine art and the commercial art worlds. This was my motivation in putting the book together. I am grateful for the opportunity to shed light on just a few of the many illustrators who see themselves as artists and I hope that after reading and looking through this book, you will see illustration in a whole new light.

EKTA

Who are you? I'm a 33-year-old artist living in Gothenburg, Sweden, with my girlfriend and son. I paint and draw and mainly work as an artist painting walls and canvas, but I also do illustration work. I have a studio in a space I share with six other artists — it's called ORO. It also works as a non-profit gallery and art venue. We've had it since 2005.

What is your biggest temptation? Dead white space. Staring at a blank wall, paper, or canvas, trying to visualize the start of an image. I don't like to plan things: content and compositions always come through the process of just adding and taking away. It's like the empty space will often help me to see how and where to begin. Sometimes you find content during or after the process and sometimes not, either way can be good. If I do commissioned illustration work I might be a little bit more aware of a subject, but preferably not too much. I find it a lot harder to work from a brief, it disturbs me a bit. Blank space and no directions are better!

Why are things the way they are? Because when I was younger I didn't understand that being an artist is not really possible. I was stupid enough to go with my heart. I'm happy to be that naive...art came through skateboarding and to me there are clear parallels between the two. In the end, drawing and painting took over completely. I try to be as versatile as possible, swapping between different media and working on several pieces at once. That way I don't get bored with stuff — if something doesn't work I can take a break from it and continue working on something else.

Where do you find peace? In most places if I'm with my family. I need to have the creative bit too and it takes a little more planning when you have a family. I usually work between nine and four from Monday to Friday (when my son is in pre-school). It's important for me to plan the

day so I stop at a stage in the process where I'm happy. If I fail then it's a little harder to find peace when I'm with my family. I'm restless by nature.

When will you be happy? I am happy, but there are many things I hate. Making stuff helps me deal with these things. I'm happy to be doing what I love every day. I probably process a lot of things I dislike in life when I'm in the studio, even though I don't really think consciously about issues I might have at the moment. I rarely get frustrated when I'm working: sometimes it's a battle but most of the time it's almost meditative. I think it will show in the piece if you have enjoyed the process but there should be traces of a little bit of struggle too, like you've experienced and gone through something with the work.

How do you know when to stop? Time will tell or you will simply run out of time. I think I've worked over a lot of stuff in the past and I'm probably a little better at knowing when something is finished. I think it's to do with being more secure and confident in my work. It takes a little more to keep things simple.

THESE PAGES AND OVERLEAF: "This series is called 'figures': they're A3 format, spray paint on paper collages. There wasn't a client as they were artwork I made in 2011 for an exhibition of my work."

OLIMPIA ZAGNOLI

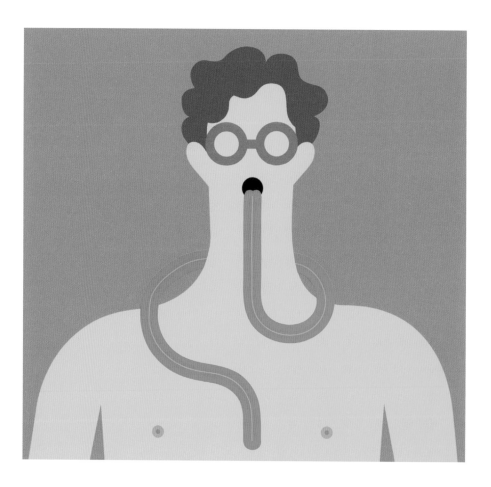

Who are you? I'm Olimpia Zagnoli. I do illustrations and then I do other things. I like The Beatles when they were in India, sending postcards, and Coca-Cola. I live in Milan and I would like to have a pig, although perhaps not because I'm not very friendly with animals.

What is your biggest temptation? To jump from one wall to another. To eat all the cake. To take some risks.

Why are things the way they are? The dishes are still in the sink because I had to focus more on my happiness.

Where do you find peace? In front of the Pacific Ocean in December. And in a few other places where I can't use my hands to check my phone.

When will you be happy? When I have a house with a bow window, a studio with trees outside, and maybe a baby.

How do you know when to stop? When my eyes turn around like a merry-go-round. I like my job very much so it's hard sometimes to turn the lights off and say "Buona notte".

ABOVE: **Toy Boy**, an article about oral sex, *Internazionale* magazine, 2012
OPPOSITE: **The Good Guide To Living Better**, *Good* magazine, 2010

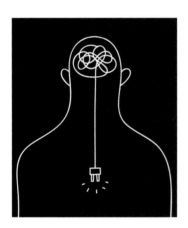

CLOCKWISE, FROM THE TOP: **Where Do We Come From?**, *Internazionale* magazine, 2011; **Illustration for the Italian festival "Balla coi Cinghiali,"** 2011; **Is Technology Unhinging our Brain?**, The *New York Times*, 2008 OPPOSITE: **Sunday Dialogue: The Old, the Young and Medicare**, The *New York Times Sunday Review*, 2011

16

JAMES JIRAT PATRADOON

Who are you? I'm James Jirat Patradoon. I'm an artist living in Sydney, Australia. I spend my time going between illustration projects and art projects. My work is mostly influenced by cyberpunk, bikers, The Undertaker, and the book *Neuromancer*. I drink a lot of coffee, and I work best at night. My favorite thing to do is sleep in.

What is your biggest temptation? My biggest temptation is to waste time: I love staying up just doing nothing. I've imposed rules on myself like no video consoles, no television. I excel at watching days pass by and doing nothing, it's scary. I'm not really allowed to do that stuff anymore.

Why are things the way they are? The number of people who don't care outweighs the number of people who do care. The reptiles want us this way, they've planned it for centuries, they want us lazy.

Where do you find peace? When I'm doing the laundry, or lacing up my shoes, or walking home. When I'm nowhere near a computer, when I don't have access to any communication, when I'm as far away from Facebook or Tumblr as possible!

When will you be happy? When I get everything I want, which includes getting rid of a lot of stuff I already have. I want to be light, I want to be free, most of all I want to be Batman.

How do you know when to stop? I stopped for a while this year when things went really dark for me. Up until that point I hadn't known what it was like to really not want to do this stuff anymore, I always assumed I'd want to do it forever. I recovered, but I don't know how, which is unsettling because if it happens again I won't know how to fix it.

ALPHA MALE

ABOVE: **Alpha Male**, personal work, digital illustration, 2010
OPPOSITE: **Untitled**, Trashbags, Sydney, digital illustration, 2010
FOLLOWING PAGES, LEFT: **Math Metal 2**, personal work, digital illustration, 2010
FOLLOWING PAGES, RIGHT: **Final Boss**, Foot Locker Art Prize Australia, digital illustration, 2011

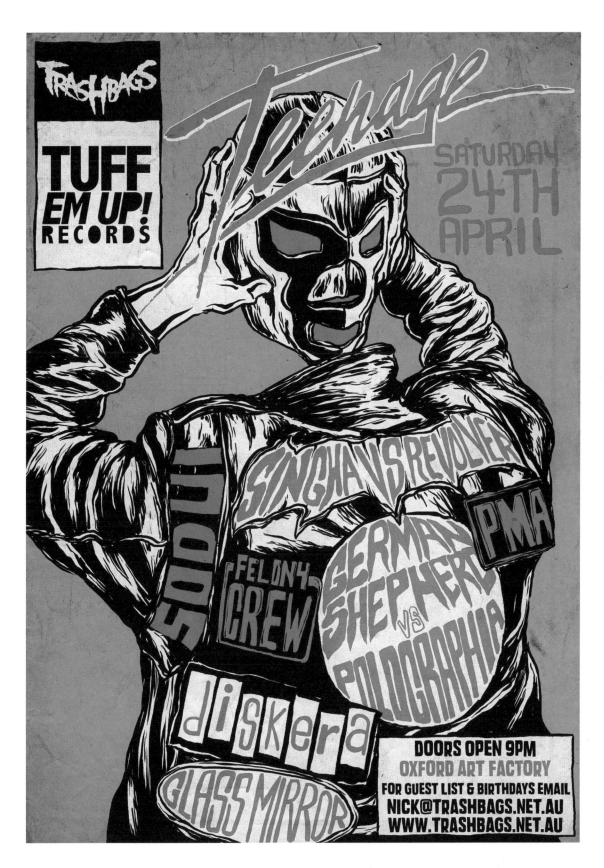

19

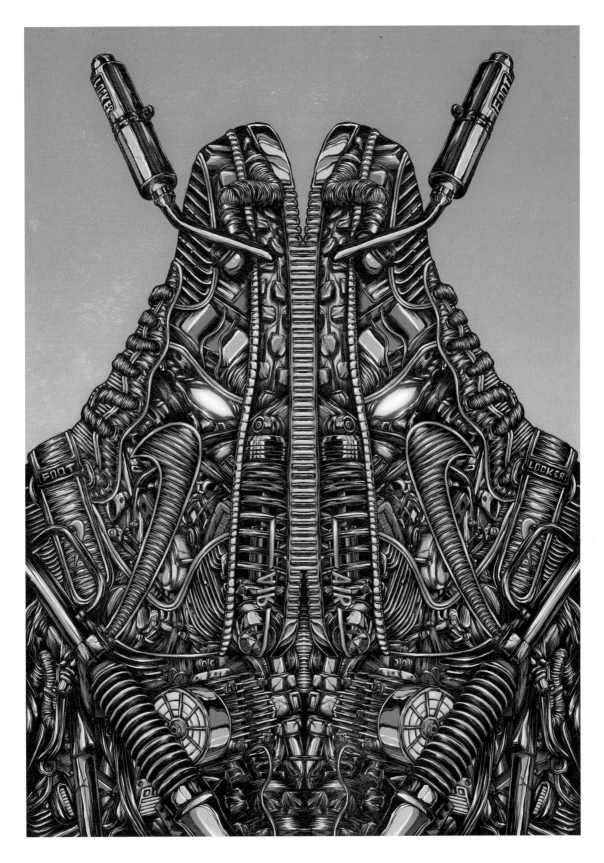

BENJAMIN MARRA

ABOVE: **Fantomah Meets Madame Satan**, personal work, mixed media, 2006
OPPOSITE: **Zombie Traci Lords**, personal work, mixed media, 2006
FOLLOWING PAGES, LEFT, ABOVE: **Cobra**, personal work, mixed media, 2006
FOLLOWING PAGES, LEFT, BELOW: **Barbarian Conquest**, personal work, mixed media, 2006
FOLLOWING PAGES, RIGHT: **Forbidden Love Behind Bars**, *Mammal* magazine, graphite and watercolor, 2007

Who are you? Benjamin Marra. I write and draw comic books and publish them through my publishing company Traditional Comics.

What is your biggest temptation? Books. I can't resist buying books, sci-fi novels, detective novels, sword-and-sorcery novels, books of art, comic books drawn by artists I admire, comic books by artists I hate but secretly love.

Why are things the way they are? Human nature. We're a doomed species.

Where do you find peace? In drawing, in conceiving story ideas, in writing comic books, in completing a project.

When will you be happy? I am happy. My life is great and very full. When will I be satisfied? Probably never. When I make a piece of art I'm happy with? But that is unlikely to occur. Not being satisfied is what propels us to keep making things. I would like to produce a longer format work next.

How do you know when to stop? When it feels right. Usually I'm wrong, though. After something is in print I usually realize what I needed to do next. But those are things apparent only to me. And it helps me to improve, when I learn from the small mistakes.

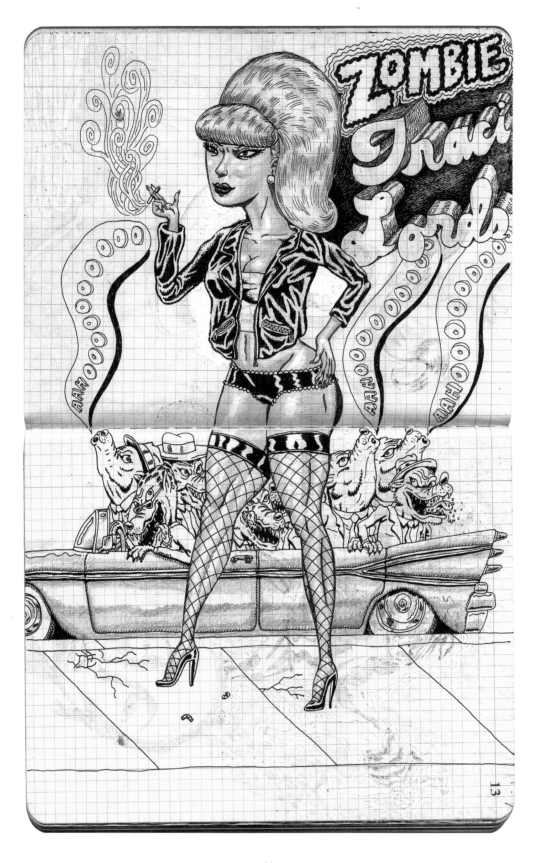

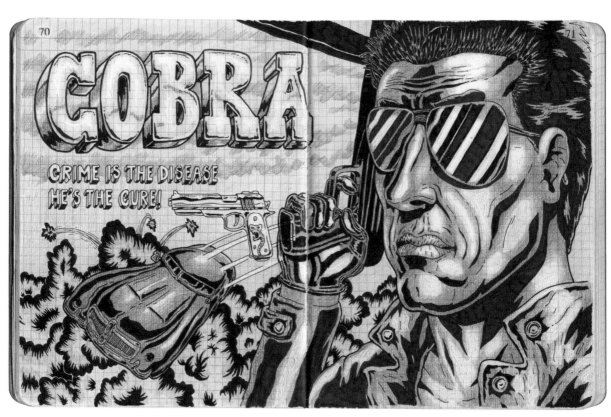

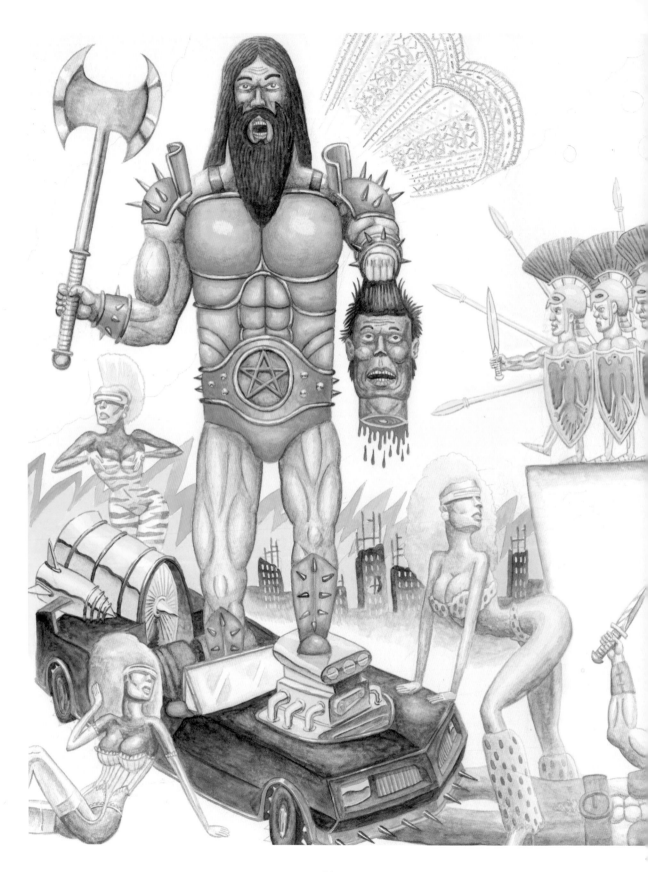

Hjellhjammer the Heschienne,
Mammal magazine, graphite
and watercolor, 2007

WHITNEY SHERMAN

Who are you? I am ridiculously above board, a straight shooter. I secretly love corny, while also loving smart humour and ideas. I'm your best friend if you play your cards right. I like to spend my money when it makes me or someone else happy. I'm a snob who dislikes snobs. And I am full of contradictions. I have what is called a "blended" family. Unusual circumstances seem to be a hallmark of my life.

What is your biggest temptation? I am tempted to tell you what I think or to act on my worst instincts, which is sometimes the same thing.

Why are things the way they are? I think about this all the time. Call me when you have the answer to this question!

Where do you find peace? When I am gardening or pushing dirt, if I am lucky enough be out there when the air is crisp and the geese are migrating. When I see something I've planted grow, turn bright green each spring, and change over the years. When I see my daughter being confident and joyful – then I forget my parental anxiety and worries.

When will you be happy? I have been and will be. Asking this question assumes too much of the wrong thing.

How do you know when to stop? I use my intuition!

ABOVE LEFT: **Burka Cocktail**, The *New York Times*, 2005
ABOVE RIGHT: **Prometheus & Copernicus**, The Templeton Foundation, digital, 2010
OPPOSITE, CLOCKWISE FROM TOP LEFT: **Guns and Youth**, *Johns Hopkins* magazine, graphite and digital, 2008; **Remembering Rochefort-en-terre**, personal work, digital and photography, 2006; **Work/Play**, Delaware College of Art and Design, ink and digital, 2010; **100 Heads for Haiti**, 100 Heads for Haiti fundraiser, collage, 2010

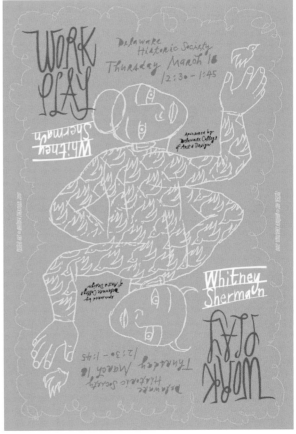

ABOVE: **How We Eat**, *Time* magazine, graphite and digital, 2009
OPPOSITE: **Reading is the Gateway to Learning**,
Williams College, graphite, digital, and photography, 2009

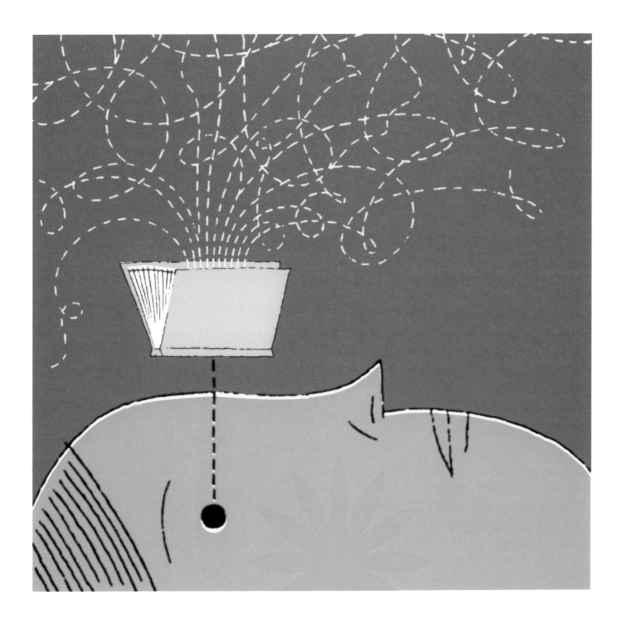

JOSEPHIN
RITSCHEL

Who are you? I am Josephin Ritschel. I was born and raised in Potsdam, a small city near Berlin. When I was a young girl my sister and I had a lot of pets and I really enjoyed spending time with them. I felt comfortable with these small animals, but then the time came when it was uncool to have guinea pigs and I felt a bit sheepish about it. Since that time I haven't grown that much and I often feel underestimated. That's why I always try to become larger than I am. Often I draw things that touched me when I was young and then everything becomes the same size as before.

What is your biggest temptation?
Sometimes I think about living outside the city in the countryside and building everything myself and needing nothing more than nature. But at the same time I am very afraid of this. The silence and the loneliness could make me go crazy, maybe.

Why are things the way they are? Because we want them as they are. We notice things as we think we know them and not as they really are. That's why everyone can see something totally different in the same thing. The things that surround us represent us in the same way. What I mean is that everyone could see what is in his head because that's what he notices in his environment.

Where do you find peace? I can find peace quite easily when I'm cycling. For me, it is the perfect locomotion. You are outside and still alone. If it was possible I would cycle everywhere.

When will you be happy? I am happy.

How do you know when to stop? Mostly my body tells me my limit. If I feel lazy I start to work or do some other activity and if I feel tired I relax. It depends on what my body says.

PRECEDING PAGES: **Future Pferde/Future Horses**, pencil on paper, 2012
OPPOSITE: **Illustration for BuHu exhibition poster**, ink on paper, 2010 CLOCKWISE, FROM TOP LEFT: **Donda**, book illustration, pencil on paper, 2011; **For Le Petit Néant**, pencil on paper, 2011; **Panther**, pencil study for mural, A4, paper, 2011

JORDAN AWAN

Who are you? I'm a 27-year-old artist, animal lover, and avid reader based in Greenpoint, Brooklyn. I draw comics, paint, and occasionally write. I co-founded Springtime Studio Illustration with my wife and fellow artist Morgan Elliott. By day, I work as an art director and designer at The *New Yorker*.

What is your biggest temptation? A stack of brand new hardcover books, a half-imagined Platonic ideal of a farmhouse in the country, expensive clothing, skipping work, and going to the beach, doing nothing.

Why are things the way they are? Hidden within the question is a sort of comforting answer: if things were otherwise, it would be otherwise. Most of it is just perception and interpretation anyway.

Where do you find peace? Relaxing at home at night with Morgan, listening to Miles Davis with the windows open and three sleeping cats scattered throughout the room.

When will you be happy? Happiness waxes and wanes like everything else. It's good to be happy and it's fine to be working to get there.

How do you know when to stop? Luckily, I have a deadline for most projects. Otherwise, it's hard to know. I have a ritual of stepping away and returning a few minutes later for a fresh look; then repeating that process several times until I feel secure with how it's feeling. Anyway, stopping is easy compared to starting.

ABOVE: **The I.Q. Gap: Culture Trumps Genes**, The *New York Times*, ink on paper, 2007
OPPOSITE, CLOCKWISE FROM TOP LEFT: **Couple**, acrylic on canvas, 2011; **Girl**, for the Kingsboro Press, ink on paper, 2007; **Couple in Bed**, personal work, acrylic on canvas, 2010

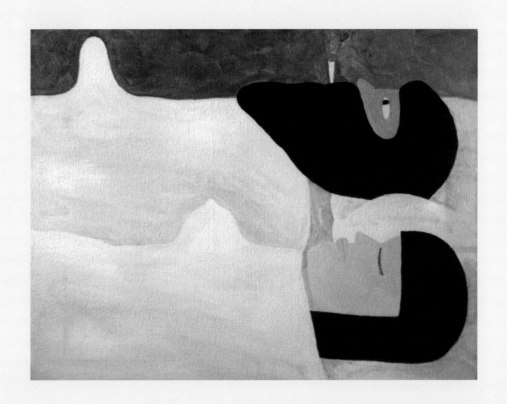

ABOVE: **The Widening Scandal in the Church,** The *New York Times*, pen and ink, 2010
OPPOSITE: **Untitled Drawing of a Man,** personal work, graphite on paper, 2008

JAN FELIKS KALLWEJT

Who are you? Not sure yet, every time I'm almost done defining myself I realize it's out of date and I have to start over.

What is your biggest temptation? Standard things: drugs, sex and rock 'n' roll.

Why are things the way they are? It's random. It's just coincidence that they are the way they are.

Where do you find peace? When I sleep, if I have a good dream.

When will you be happy? When I'm able to realize that I already am.

How do you know when to stop? When I notice it's more than enough.

ABOVE AND OPPOSITE: **Prints**, for Miligram Gallery exhibition, 2009

ABOVE AND OPPOSITE: **JFK Maps,**
digital prints, 2009

GERARD ARMENGOL

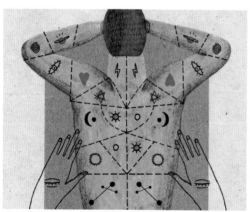

Who are you? Gerard Armengol.

What is your biggest temptation? White. White things. White as beginnings. White as a shape generator.

Why are things the way they are? Because we made all those things.

Where do you find peace? Breaking white. Noising.

When will you be happy? When poetic justice exists.

How do you know when to stop? When you decide to show up.

CLOCKWISE, FROM TOP LEFT: **Flaming Volcano**, personal work, ink, 2011; **The Beach**, personal work, colored pencil, and marker, 2009; **True Love**, for Gran Amant's "El Primer Disc," Foehn Records, ink, color ink, and marker, 2011; **At Her Fingertips**, The *New York Times*, mixed media, 2010
OPPOSITE: **Stanley Brinks**, Primeros Pasitos, mixed media, 2009

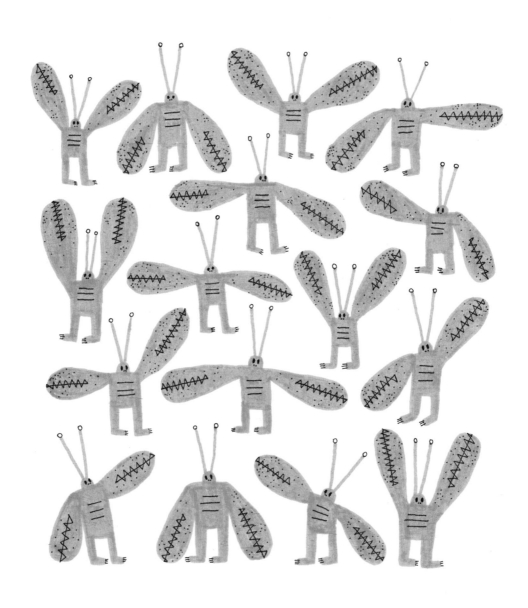

ABOVE: **Illustration for DeVotchKa poster**,
Alternatilla, mixed media, 2009
OPPOSITE: **Sweater**, Equilibriste and Platovacío,
Alternatilla, gouache, marker, and ink, 2009

Untitled, personal work, acrylic, crayon, ink, and pencil, 2010

PAUL BLOW

Who are you? Paul Blow, illustrator and wooden house builder.

What is your biggest temptation? At the moment, a Makita power drill with 1,000 50mm screws—it's a builder's thing.

Why are things the way they are? Because if they were not then I would be a carpenter...but not the walking on water kind.

Where do you find peace? Never, I suffer from mild tinnitus.

When will you be happy? When I've finished the house and my hearing gets better.

How do you know when to stop? When my bleeding eyes, ears, and nose tell me to.

ABOVE LEFT: **Colum McCann**, *Usbek & Rica*, mixed media and digital, 2010
ABOVE RIGHT: **Art Buyer**, *Evolver* magazine, mixed media and digital, 2010
OPPOSITE: **Wild One**, *Evolver* magazine, mixed media, 2010

CLOCKWISE, FROM TOP LEFT: **Bleeding Eyes**, *3 x 3* magazine,
mixed media and digital, 2008; **Gods & Monsters**, Nobrow, mixed
media, 2010; **Seasons of Ash**, The *New York Times*, mixed media, 2010
OPPOSITE: **The Modern Fix**, The *Independent*, mixed media, 2012

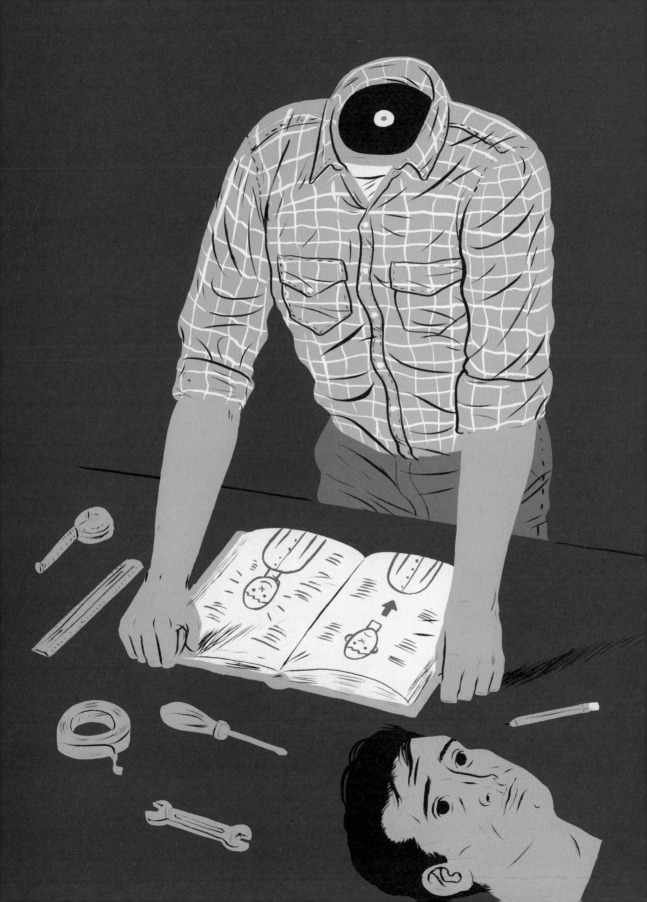

Ekta & Olimpia Zagnoli
on *Speed*

 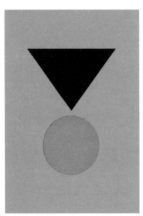  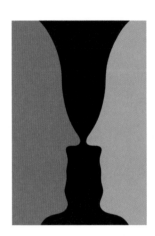

What does speed mean to you?

Ekta: Speed makes me think of Amphetamine, the drug of choice for the people who steal copper cables. I often meet these guys as we have a common interest in abandoned buildings. I look for places to paint and they need a quiet place to burn the cables in order to get the copper out.

Olimpia Zagnoli: Speed, to me, is being late for a train.

Did working with your collaborator change your view on the theme?

E: Yes, I think Olimpia's work brings a really good flow to how you read the order of the images. Her work is really reduced, too, which helped me cut back a bit. Sometimes I make things a little more difficult than they have to be.

OZ: Definitely, my interpretation of the theme is a sequence of images running one after the other. Ekta, to me, looks more focused on speed as change.

How did you find working together?

E: We decided on a format and divided the space so that our images would read in a narrative way. I made the first image,

which I see as a figure trying to move forward quickly, but it's being held back by a strong wind. I sent it to Olimpia and the process pretty much started rolling.

OZ: We talked a bit about the theme and decided not to be too literal. Then we organized the space we had and divided it. Each of us had a slice of a page and we started working on that. Ekta sent me his first works and I sent him mine. It was easy!

Did you learn something about yourself?

E: Yes, it reminded me of how good it is for your creative process to do collaborations. I did a lot of collaborative work in the past and really enjoyed it, but I haven't done any in a while. Most of the time you're on your own with what you're doing and it's cool to share a process with another person.

OZ: Sure. I've learnt that I can work with other people on the same piece and actually love the result.

Will this affect your future work?

E: I think it will for sure. It reminded me of the importance of reduction.

OZ: Yes, I'm gonna be an astronaut.

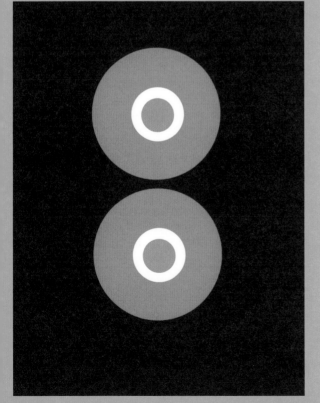

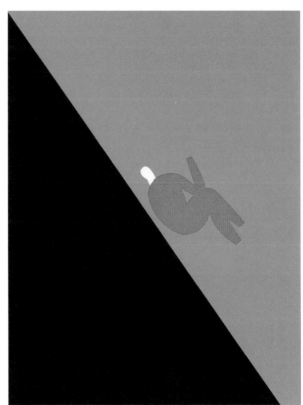

James Jirat Patradoon & Benjamin Marra on *Beauty*

What does beauty mean to you?

James Jirat Patradoon: Our theme was beauty, and throughout the process of the collaboration we had different ways of looking at it. Originally, we were going to do scenarios full of superficial people, in night clubs, and on dirty street corners. I think that's how beauty is "used" on a regular basis, as something to entice, a façade. We ended up changing the idea to focus on specific characters, and then we started looking at beauty as something more specific, being in the eye of the beholder – the idea that no matter how strange something was, there was something else out there in the world that would be attracted to it, so we started to draw majestic odd couples.

Benjamin Marra: The term beauty reminds me of the old adage "Beauty is in the eye of the beholder," what is beautiful to one may not be beautiful to another. It makes me think of attraction, earthly delights in a visual nature and what's appealing to the sense of sight in our plane of existence.

Did working with your collaborator change your view on the theme?

JJP: Yeah, Benjamin was drawing some very strange unexpected stuff, which was exactly what we were trying to explore. I drew the hand monster, and Benjamin responded with that camel thing – who's to say it couldn't happen? Then he drew the old lady with two children on her shoulders, so I responded with what I thought her husband would look like, an urn of ashes with a speakerbox attached so he could still talk.

BM: Slightly. We changed our stroke midstream, opting for a different approach as to how to respond to our theme. Instead of drawing scenes of beauty in decay, we created characters who were lovers, who were beautiful possibly in each other's eyes.

How did you find working together?

JJP: It was hard to maintain momentum across the globe and with our own busy schedules. The way I always try to do these things is to get an idea open enough for both people, and then just let them go away and tinker on it on their own. I think illustrators spend a lot of time alone so they do their best work

alone. It was hard, but I'm happy with how the conversation turned out, I think we would have gotten lost had we stuck to doing complex street scenes.

BM: It was a privilege and an honor to work with James. I think we immediately found our sensibilities meshed seamlessly even though our work is somewhat different. We had several conversations over email about our approach. We focused mainly on how our collaboration would function. Initially, we both wanted to work on the same image, have our drawings mixed in the same frame, but that proved too inefficient so we opted for doing individual pieces which were responses to the other's work.

Did you learn something about yourself?

JJP: I learnt that images can still go wrong, I had to redraw urn head about three times. At one point it was the Sarcophagus of Tutankhamun, and then it changed back, and then I had to redraw its clothes to match the line width used for its head. I don't know how I became such a perfectionist. I spent a lot of time trying to work on different color schemes as well but it turned out to be strongest in black and white. Sometimes you just don't know how an image is going to turn out.

BM: Not really. I know my process very well now and have done a lot of experimenting in the past with different approaches. I've done many collaborations – some more successful than others. Working with James was very easy and makes me believe collaborations can create results that are greater than the sum of their parts.

Will this affect your future work?

JJP: This kind of thing really sneaks up on you. I don't want it to happen again, especially on a client job or something, but I think sometimes it's good when you end up with something unexpected, there is a bit more of a process. It's not a very neat or organized way of making images, and I spent most of the time feeling anxious about it, but I like how it turned out.

BM: I think that's unlikely, but I might be more open in the future to certain collaborations. I'm pretty set in my ways.

Whitney Sherman & Josephin Ritschel on *Excess*

What does excess mean to you?

Whitney Sherman: Excess is going beyond what is needed to what is desired, or to go beyond to a place without limits. In some cases, for some people, going to excess has a deep level of pleasure, it gives a sense of being free. Without judging excess as a choice, certain ecstasies not found in the day to day are reached. In nature, each extreme is compensated by a reciprocating extreme. This principle is good to know when making choices about one's excesses.

Josephin Ritschel: When I was thinking about excess, first of all pork feasts or sex orgies came into my mind. Excess for me is when people take more of something than is good for them. I also liked the idea of showing different eccentric people.

Did working with your collaborator change your view on the theme?

WS: My views are always changed by watching other artists think. I've always been interested in how other people think, how they view things – whether I agree, disagree, or am ambivalent about their views. At times there can be a radical shift in my paradigm. While working with Josephin, I noticed more of what we thought in common than differences. I was mostly intrigued by her visual perspective rather than her politics.

JR: After I saw her first drawing I realized that we have kind of the same mood in the picture. I mean we kept them calm and kind of self-contained. Maybe somebody else would make more of an action illustration for an excess picture.

How did you find working together?

WS: Josephin and I are both busy, but were very invested in the idea of getting to know each other better. Our email conversations were brief, thoughtful, and playful. I really enjoyed getting to know her because I admire her work!

JR: We decided to mix our two ideas, so we had two variations on the theme and each of us replied to the other's first drawing. Whitney chose a body adornment like tattooing and I chose a collecting excess. After we finished our first sketches we swapped the drawings so the other person got an idea of what it would look like and we started with the second one. My answer to Whitney's first image was the other body excess: bodybuilding. She chose a collecting girl. It was important to us that people could see where the collaboration was happening.

Did you learn something about yourself?

WS: After making years' worth of imagery, there are still more stories to tell.

JR: It was great to see how somebody else works on the same theme. This meant I could reflect my own drawing better.

Will this affect your future work?

WS: As I have said, after making years' worth of imagery, there are still more stories to tell.

JR: It is great to work on a good theme that somebody else has told me about. And, of course, it can be a good experience to work with somebody you haven't seen before. And I can say it was. I would do it again immediately.

Jordan Awan &
Jan Feliks Kallwejt
on *Winter*

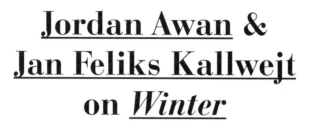

What does winter mean to you?

Jordan Awan: Winter can be the hardest season to get through. I've begun to enjoy it more over the past few years, though. I like staying indoors, relaxing in my apartment. I think it was school more than winter that made me dread the season when I was younger.

Jan Feliks Kallwejt: Season of the year seems to be quite an easy subject, so the trick is not to do something banal with it. I just thought about it as a state of mind.

Did working with your collaborator change your view on the theme?

JA: Since Jan is from a much colder climate originally, our experiences of winter must be very different. My first drawing was more about my personal experience of winter in New York – cozy late nights spent hiding from the weather – and Jan's was almost an anthropomorphized version of winter, a sort of yeti monster. His took place outdoors, and was about having fun in the landscape; mine was about escaping the same outdoors and having fun inside.

JFK: It's so much fun to see what another creative person can come up with, thinking about the same theme. After seeing the first illustration from Jordan I was inspired and many new ideas came into my mind, although I stuck to my first vision.

How did you find working together?

JA: Because of a time-zone difference and how busy we were, Jan and I made a few failed attempts to connect over video chat. He expressed his typical discomfort with collaborations, which I can identify with to some extent too. Eventually we decided we both felt comfortable doing one complete image by ourselves, then sending them to each other and making a response piece.

JFK: We are both rather busy so communication was not that smooth. At the beginning we decided that instead of discussing everything we would just talk with images. I prepared one piece, so did Jordan and then in our second illustration we both tried to combine our first image with the image of our collaborator.

Did you learn something about yourself?

JA: I think I learn something about myself during every project, though it might be difficult to nail down exactly what. Perhaps the most interesting part was seeing Jan draw my characters.

JFK: I've always known that it's easier for me to work alone, I just realized it's fun to collaborate and think it would be cool to do it more often, even against my creative preferences.

Will this affect your future work?

JA: I'm sure it will! It's always shocking to see your own imagery rendered by someone else – to see their approach and aesthetic come through.

JFK: It will probably be easier to do some teamwork with other illustrators in the future.

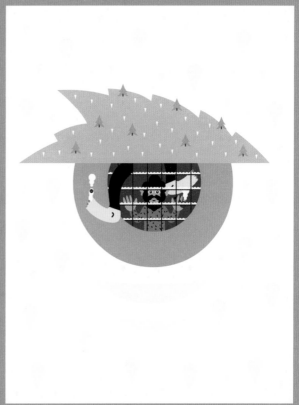

Gerard Armengol & Paul Blow on *Party*

What does party mean to you?

Gerard Armengol: La Joie de Vivre. Energy against physics, creating, and destroying. Ourselves, outer spaces. Dangerous ritual. Dark side of the moon. Fiction. Pulpdream.

Paul Blow: The theme of party can mean many things to me, but in particular how people interact with one another. Often I see people in groups sitting together all interacting, not with each other, but with their phones, I mean what's that about? I don't own a mobile phone, but if I did, would I be invited to these "virtual" parties? I hope not. I like eye-to-eye contact.

Did working with your collaborator change your view on the theme?

GA: It had a cohesion effect. All the drawings we put together formed a "based on a true story" composition.

PB: In some ways, yes, it became less about the theme and more about cutting and pasting – having fun, as you might do at a party...a cutting up and pasting party.

How did you find working together?

GA: I had fun. It was difficult at the beginning but successful in the end. Also difficult because of the distance between Paul and me, plus the electronic communication. This is always causing problems between humans.

PB: Time constraints on me at the moment are big – simply because I'm running a business, building a house and raising a family, so direct email conversations were limited, which actually suited me fine. Conversations took place within the exchange of ideas and emotions simply through the images. Gerard bravely started with a simple drawing and then I responded with something that was part of some recent art I'd been working on. I developed a collage way of working with bits and pieces of work lying around on my hard drive. Re-contextualizing them gave them new meaning and new powers which I found both inspiring and playful. The sense of play and happy serendipity was extremely liberating for me as my normal work routine demands tight briefs and specific final outcomes. I was having a party and losing my inhibitions.

Did you learn something about yourself?

GA: Yes, no more party.

PB: Only to reinforce my belief that experimentation must always be at the heart of what an artist is trying to achieve... either in grand gestures or in small incremental steps. It's all a journey.

Will this affect your future work?

GA: Yes, definitely.

PB: Possibly. I think the collaging and working with less and developing more abstract pieces could be exciting, specifically looking at the working process and simplifying it, working more intuitively and playing!

Fig. 12.

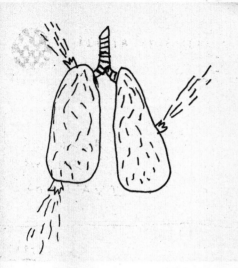

PAUL PAETZEL

Who are you? I am Paul Paetzel. I was born in Berlin, Germany, where I still live and work. After I graduated from school I started to study illustration. I finished in December 2010. My diploma work was a comic called "Die Geschichte von Rudolf". It is a story about a comic artist facing his deepest fears. Rudolf is my alter ego. I use this character to tell stories about different things that bother me or touched me in the past. My final year project was published by Edition Biografiktion which is a very small publishing house I founded together with Ana Albero and Till Hafenbrak, two of my very best friends. Working together with them is so much fun. I can't think of something better at the moment. I spend a lot of time drawing. Just sometimes I feel a bit bad when I realize that my horizon is mainly focused on illustration and comics, but the truth is that this is what I am interested in the most.

What is your biggest temptation? I guess that I am a very good eater. If I find something tasty then it is difficult for me not to eat it up very quickly. Chocolate bars disappear immediately after I open them up. I often try to eat more slowly, but if food is delicate it is most fulfilling for me to finish it in a fast way. I never go to the supermarket with an empty stomach because I would buy too much stuff that I won't need in the end.

Why are things the way they are? I think that there is an infinite number of possibilities of how things can be. If 100 people draw exactly the same object all the images will look completely different in the end because everybody sees the object in a different way.

Where do you find peace? I find peace in normal activities like enjoying a good movie or drinking a beer with some friends. I think in those moments I am not concentrating on myself which is good. One reason for not finding peace is that I listen too much to myself, so sometimes small problems become bigger. When I try not to worry too much I am much happier.

When will you be happy? Most of the time I feel neutral. I am happy when somebody makes a good joke. I am also happy if somebody laughs at my jokes.

How do you know when to stop? To know when to start something and when to stop it is a very important part of success. The right timing is always good, I would say. Sometimes I start too early or I stop too late, but if I realize that I am not enjoying the things I usually enjoy anymore then I stop for sure.

ABOVE: **Limones**, the Baure documentation project, pencil, 2010
OPPOSITE: **Day and Night**, Nobrow, ink and Photoshop, 2010

OPPOSITE: **The City**, *Human News* 2, silkscreen, 2010
ABOVE LEFT: **Portrait of UNS**, UNS, ink and Photoshop, 2010
ABOVE RIGHT: **Zazie dans le métro**, unpublished illustration for
Büchergilde Gutenberg, pencil, 2010

IRKUS M. ZEBERIO

Who are you? Irkus is my real name, not a pseudonym. Master artist. Drawing to search. To build and own everything I desire.

What is your biggest temptation?
My biggest temptation is meat.

Why are things the way they are? At atomic level, the protons are 0.14% less massive than neutrons. This is a universal constant. That's why there are wars.

Where do you find peace? Facing the sea at night. Winter. Strong wind, light and persistent rain. Breaking waves.

When will you be happy? When I finish all my projects. Never.

How do you know when to stop?
It's different for a story or for a drawing. At the comic, time moves through the pages, it's difficult to stop. I usually just give up at a time when everything seems to square with the tertiary Aristotelian scheme. Assuming that nothing ever ends, the end is the beginning. In a drawing, time limits are on the page, it is difficult to find the right time. But you have a clear finish, the limits of a plane. So you have to work with composition, colors, etc. The intuition can leave you far from the objective, and destroy the picture or just leave you fantastically at the apex, with sub-atomic precision, in a magical place. The reason leaves you at a safe distance, but not magical enough.

ABOVE: **"Biziko gara horrela hirurehun bat urtez, banku guztietako jabetzaren kaltez,"** part of a work based on Dizzy Gillespie's music for an exhibition about jazz, digital pencil on digital paper, 2010
OPPOSITE ABOVE: **"Si vis pacem para bellum,"** personal work, digital pencil on digital paper, 2011
OPPOSITE BELOW: **"Little big men,"** personal work, digital pencil on digital paper, 2011

OPPOSITE: **"Jules Karnibal 2,"** Ass. Les Golfes,
digital pencil on digital paper, 2012
ABOVE: **"El boig del cavall,"** Bedroom music band,
digital pencil on digital paper, 2011

ZELOOT

Bowling It was a poster designed for my Helbaard companion who organized an evening of concerts at a bowling centre in Brussels. I wanted it to show the surrealness of the event and to do something detailed after making a series of posters that were simple and very graphic. I felt like drawing a lot without thinking much about where it should go, for a change.

Fat Worms I more or less started with illustration and the whole poster thing when the Garage, a venue in the Hague, called and asked me to design a flyer for their monthly concerts. I had studied painting at art school six years before but had kind of given up on the idea of creating art. I didn't feel my opinions or visions were worthwhile enough and graphic design didn't interest me because I considered it too much of a purely aesthetic discipline. When I started to create flyers and posters for the Garage, I really enjoyed expressing myself through something as abstract as music, "representing" so many different kinds of music that I felt free to change form, style, etc., every time – something you hardly see in the art scene or illustration world. Besides there wasn't an art director giving me restrictions and my name or identity wasn't important. This poster was used as a poster and cut up as flyers (with the info about the concert printed on the back).

Ariel Pink This is one of my first silkscreened posters. Because of Ariel Pink's eclectic style, with influences such as 60s garage, psych 70s funk, and electronic pop, I tried to bring some of these era characteristics together visually.

Sonic Youth It was great to make a poster for a show that was partly about Sonic Youth's great interest and support of unknown artists on the underground scene. I had made different posters for musicians and bands that I had played or worked with so I guess that connected them to me in some way. The posters were huge, hanging on the streets of Bolzano...quite the opposite of the little, fresh-printed ones for our own Helbaard concerts that I tried to hang on the very limited number of places available in my city of the Hague.

Deerhoof I always start by listening to the music that the poster is for and try to generate some kind of physical sensation and look for a form to visualize it. There seems to be no running model for me when I work. Sometimes I draw and erase for hours, starting from a very vague or very clear idea until there's a point of recognition. This poster design was not going to be printed by me, but in the States, so it limited my way of designing improvisationally by working on the layers in between the printing.

The Decemberists I've been designing posters for the Decemberists since 2009. It was quite a challenge to make so many posters for one band and still come up with something "new" every time. These posters are mostly influenced thematically, by their latest albums and their songs. The music style doesn't come from the same "scene" that I used to make posters for so I gave it a slightly different approach stylistically with less risky choices for the printing part since they are printed in the States. For me, it's more interesting to use the silkscreen medium not just as a reproduction technique, but also as a tool itself in the whole designing process.

HENRIK DRESCHER

Who are you? I am a visual artist, my work grows out of travel and notebook keeping. I was born in Denmark and grew up in the States. I have lived all over the world and am currently settled in China's Western Yunnan Province, with my wife Wu Wing Yee.

What is your biggest temptation? I don't really think that much about temptation. My life is full of art and music, marriage and a blind dog named Tofu.

Why are things the way they are?
Because we get what we deserve.

Where do you find peace? Lying on my couch playing the banjo.

When will you be happy? I'm content, the pursuit of happiness is for the disillusioned.

How do you know when to stop? I always stop at question number six.

ABOVE: **Personal work**
OPPOSITE: **Promotional poster for Emigre film in Mexico**, designed by Vanessa Eckstein, BLOK design

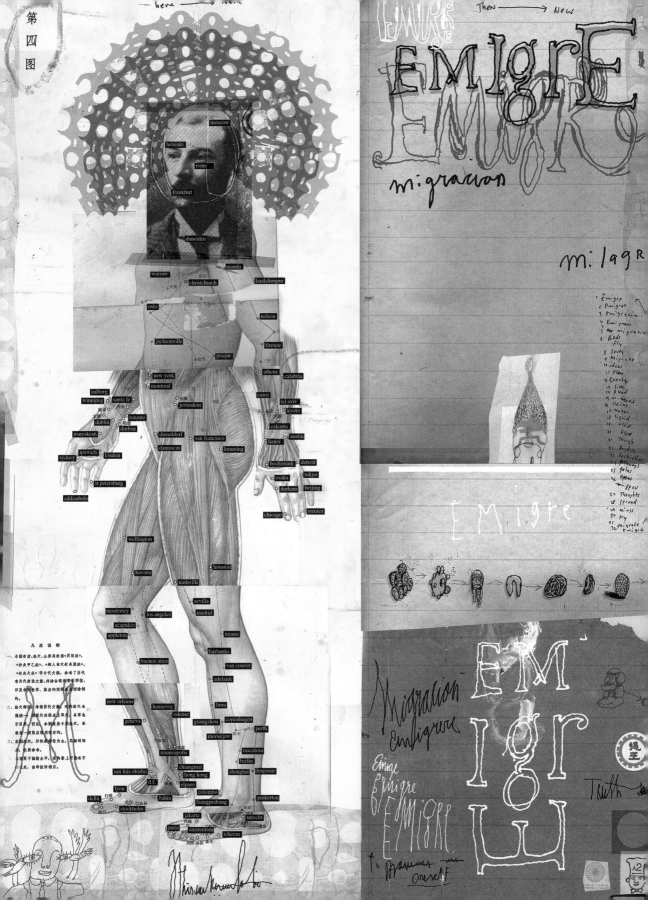

From the Start she knew that she was Counting... DISASTER

OPPOSITE: **Personal work**
ABOVE: **Personal work**

SHOBOSHOBO

Who are you? My name is Mehdi Hercberg and I'm also known as Shoboshobo. I try to live and work in Paris where I also teach in an art school. My work involves a wide range of projects including illustration, graphic artworks, clothes design, music, and printed editions. My graphic work is mainly focused on monsters and creatures that one could say are strange, pop, frightening, and sometimes cute. I have performed, done workshops, lectured and exhibited in several different countries. In particular, I have a strong bond with Japan, where I visit as often as I possibly can.

What is your biggest temptation? To go to Japan, find a booth in the mountains and just stay there making drawings...

Why are things the way they are? Things are not the way they are, that's what they want us to think.

Where do you find peace? That's not what I'm looking for.

When will you be happy? After the revolution.

How do you know when to stop? Usually, I don't.

THESE PAGES AND OVERLEAF: **Shoboshobo sweatshirt,** flock on sweatshirt

YU MATSUOKA

Who are you? I'm a Japanese girl who has been living in France and now in Belguim for almost 10 years. I quit my country home to study in Paris at the Beaux-Arts and graduated in 2006. So I'm supposed to be an artist, but I'd rather say I'm a painter. At the moment my way of expressing myself is restricted to canvases and oil colors. I also draw a lot in my numerous sketchbooks and on any paper I can find. Drawing is a way to release tension and to let out all the envies I keep inside. Painting is a slightly different process which demands more complex attention. One could say I am a figurative painter, but I would like to erase this supposed frontier which I think doesn't exist.

What is your biggest temptation? I don't know if one can really call it a temptation, but I am interested in mixing two opposite things in paintings: what is commonly accepted as beauty and its opposite, ugliness. The temptation may be there, when something I am working on becomes too pretty, for example, I feel the need to "attack" it. Being Japanese, I can't stand the word "kawaii" which is used all the time to qualify any supposedly pretty thing. I would not accept that for my work. I need to express this duality that lies in every single thing in this life. I can't avoid this in my work.

Why are things the way they are? Again, because of this duality that lies in all things in this world that makes it possible that at any moment the so-called "good" can turn into the so-called "bad". There is also this weight of the past that we always have to bear without being really able to disregard it.

Where do you find peace? I feel peace in my dog who is like a sheep and sometimes works as a pillow. Also when I'm in nature, when I'm painting, listening to music, playing the piano, taking a hot bath in onsen and eating soba, reading books, watching films.

When will you be happy? I will be happy when I am able to live with my paintings. At that time I want to go to Patagonia and Bora Bora! I would be immersed in the deep wilderness and pure violence and silence of nature far away from those mental constructions of human beings we call cities (where I live).

How do you know when to stop? I don't really know how to stop. It is something that happens and that is evident: it's the end of the story. You get tired of this thing, ready to abandon it. Sometimes you just miss the end, you've been a little bit too far and you must walk back to find that "place" again. Some other time you won't be able to go back, everything is lost. You'd better start the whole story all over again...

ABOVE: **Yellow Mountain**, marker on paper, A4
OPPOSITE, CLOCKWISE FROM TOP LEFT: **Shika**, oil on paper, 12 × 16" (30 × 40 cm), 2010; **Kazan**, marker on paper, 20 × 24" (50 × 60 cm), 2009; **Erikisa**, oil on paper, 12 × 16" (30 × 40 cm), 2010

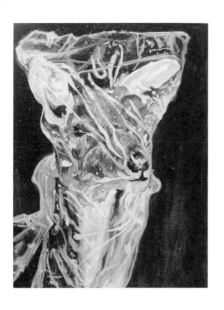

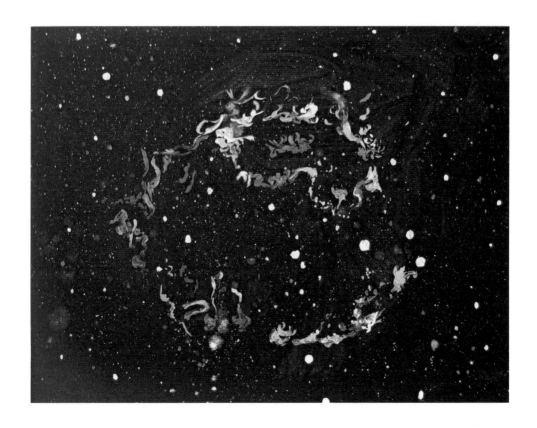

Iceberg Koori No Yama, marker on paper, A4

EDEL RODRIGUEZ

Who are you? I grew up in a small town in the Cuban countryside. I think my background informs much of my work and general outlook on life. My parents were farm and factory workers and I think I inherited some of my work ethic from them. My work is influenced by many life experiences, family, travel, music, history and politics. Cultural displacement is a theme that tends to show up in my work in a variety of ways.

What is your biggest temptation? As an artist, I get easily bored and I'm always tempted to try something new. This just seems to be my working method. I think it's my natural way of working so it's hard to think of it as a temptation.

Why are things the way they are? I think there are basic human instincts that make things the way they are: jealousy, greed, lust, anger, etc. Sometimes we try to tame these instincts, but I enjoy standing back and just watching it all take place.

Where do you find peace? I find peace in my work. In work that has no deadline or client. Just getting lost in the act of creating something without pressure can be very peaceful. Sometimes an afternoon goes by and I don't even realize it.

When will you be happy? I've usually always been happy with my work and life. Sometimes I think of family and friends who have not been as lucky as I have been and it puts things in perspective. I could have easily ended up working hard as a farm laborer so I feel very lucky to have ended up where I am.

How do you know when to stop? As it relates to work, it can be hard to know when to stop. Sometimes there are a number of paintings under a final painting because I just keep on going. Much of the time I stop when something clicks and the art in front of me feels like it's making a complete statement, whatever that may be. In personal or professional relationships, I often let the other person speak and I just listen.

ABOVE: **Luz,** acrylic on canvas, 24 × 30" (60 × 76 cm), 2010
OPPOSITE: **Perla,** acrylic on canvas, 24 × 30" (60 × 76 cm), 2010

OPPOSITE: **Warrior**, mixed media, an exhibition of Maori art, published in The *San Francisco Chronicle*, 8 × 10" (20 × 25 cm), 2005
ABOVE LEFT: **Snips**, acrylic on bark paper, book cover for *Anthills of the Savannah* by Chinua Achebe, 16 × 23" (40 × 58 cm), 2009
ABOVE RIGHT: **Vessel**, acrylic on bark paper, 16 × 23" (40 × 58 cm), 2010

DREW BECKMEYER

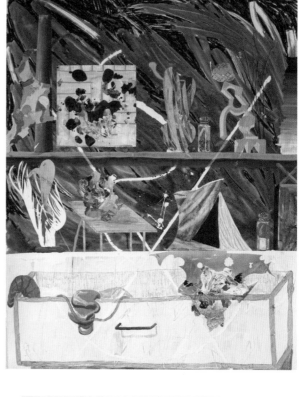

Who are you? Drew Joseph Beckmeyer, b. 1982, Los Angeles, CA, 5'10", 165 lbs. Brown hair, blue eyes. Corrective lenses.

What is your biggest temptation? To sleep my life into the gutter.

Why are things the way they are? To keep us on our toes, so we don't give up on thinking and wondering and working and trying.

Where do you find peace? Where the dog is.

When will you be happy? If I say it isn't really a priority, does that mean that I am already happy? But if I achieved happiness without some sort of ceremony or knowledge of achieving it, that would kind of make me sad. So...maybe I don't really, really understand the word.

How do you know when to stop? Stopping is one of the few things I will admit to not knowing how to do. Stopping and being positive.

ABOVE RIGHT: **10 Abstract Shapes on a Shelf in Front of a Window at Night,** mixed media on paper, 22 × 30" (56 × 76 cm), 2010
RIGHT: **Untitled,** ink and gouache on paper, 9 × 12" (23 × 30 cm), 2008
OPPOSITE: **Untitled,** mixed media on paper, 11 × 14" (28 × 36 cm), 2011

OPPOSITE: **Tower of Babel**, mixed media on paper, 20 × 22"
(51 × 56 cm), 2009
ABOVE: **Untitled**, acrylic, collage, and digital, 12 × 9"
(30 × 23 cm), 2011

AHU SULKER

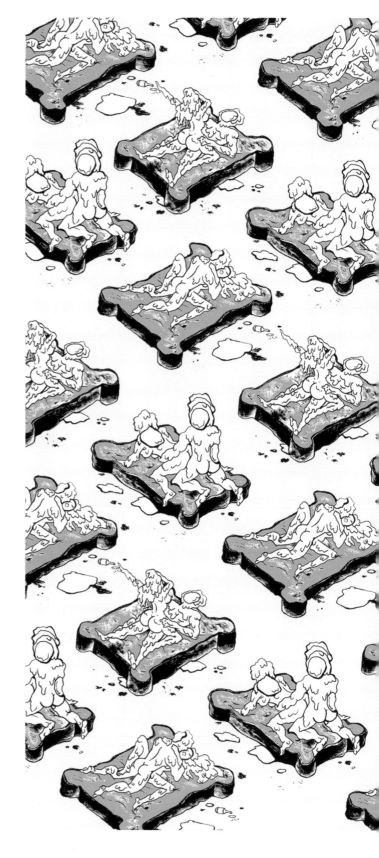

Who are you? I am a humble and sensible person. I like and judge people by the energy they give me. I am a big dreamer and I get lost in my made-up world of fairytales. I love cheesy movies and stories. My biggest passion is art but also it's my biggest struggle. I like comfort and order so I seek people who are the opposite. I get a great amount of pleasure from taking photos but I'm no photographer. I have obsessions about things just like everyone else and I don't know when to let go. Most importantly, I try to stay true to myself and the people I love.

Where do you find peace? I find peace when I am drawing at work or in my sketchbook. It's that tiny feeling you get when you stop for a second and realize you let your mind wonder somewhere else.

When will you be happy? There will never be a "when," it's a realization that happiness is how you interpret life.

Why are things the way they are? Because it was put there or it was made. Things mold a pattern and you're just a piece of it.

How do you know when to stop? It's a feeling you get deep, deep, deep inside you, but sometimes it is an illusion and it's hard to stop. Everything has a limit: it's up to you as to how much you can handle.

What is your biggest temptation?
I shamelessly love to be lazy. French fries are my favorite and I can never say no. I love to watch very cheesy movies and talk about them afterwards. But my biggest temptation is to be in bed and watch tv for hours.

Egg on Bread pattern, *Egg on Bread*
newspaper, ink drawing, 2010

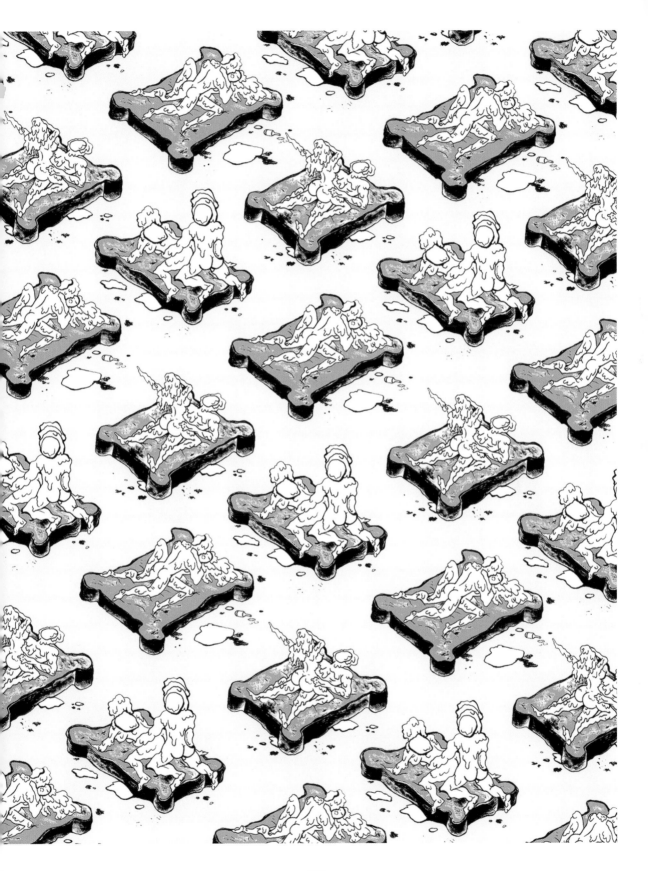

OPPOSITE: **Still**, personal work and POUNDPOUND print,
ink drawing and digital coloring, 2012
ABOVE: **The Wild**, personal work and POUNDPOUND
print, ink drawing and digital coloring, 2012

YUKO SHIMIZU

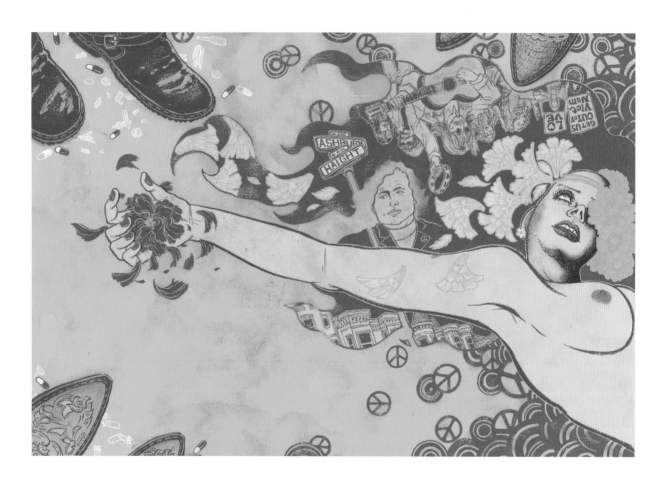

Who are you? Cogito ergo sum.

What is your biggest temptation?
Chocolate. Really good milk chocolate.

Why are things the way they are? Because you don't try to change them.

Where do you find peace? My inner self.

When will you be happy? I am generally happy because I know that life is never perfect and that is OK.

How do you know when to stop? Experience tells me.

ABOVE: "The Dark Side of the Summer of Love," *Playboy*, July 2007
OPPOSITE, CLOCKWISE FROM TOP LEFT: Portrait of Butcher Ryan Farr, client Chow.com, 2009; Portrait of Keith Richards, The *New York Times Book Review*, November 14, 2010; *New York Magazine* sex issue illustration, 2005

ABOVE: **Now Hear This!**, The *Word* magazine supplement,
CD cover, February 2009
OPPOSITE: **"Saigo Takamori,"** illustration for the book
The Beautiful and the Grotesque, 2010

Paul Paetzel
& Irkus M. Zeberio
on *Gluttony*

Paul Paetzel: Gluttony is one of the seven deadly sins, which is a very out-dated system, but still useful for finding good topics to draw. It is a very strong, but also very open word. It can lead to many different pictures because you can think of it in so many ways.

The four illustrations Irkus and I did together also show four different aspects of our topic. Each of us made two sketches which we then swapped. We had to reinterpret the rough of the other and make an illustration out of it. This process was very interesting for me because I saw two visions of Irkus and I had to write out those ideas. So I made something completely different from what I would have done if I had worked on my own.

The collaboration with Irkus was a lot of fun. I already knew and loved his work before I met him at the Ilu Station festival in Barcelona in 2011. He is a very funny and crazy guy. I am really happy that I could work with him because I could have a look at how he starts a project, how he works on it, what ideas he finds interesting and wants to realize.

What our illustrations have in common is that we wanted to present the dark and morbid side of gluttony in a humorous way.

Irkus M. Zeberio: I grew up in a place where gastronomy and cooking are very important. But this kind of culture has his own junkies. Happy drunken fatties who spend time going from one tavern to another, with no objective other than eating, drinking, and singing. Or thinking about what will they do for dinner while taking their lunch. That's gluttony for me, the inaptitude of knowing when to stop, when to know the party is over. When things become insane.

Paul enlightened me. I was inspired by Pantagruel's story and I wanted to do something more political. Looking at his sketches, he reminded me of the tavern way of life. He gave me his sense of humour and fantasy. I finally drew something more human, leaving aside the political gluttony and returning to the gourmet gluttony.

I was scared about working together with the same image. I always used to work alone and you know how big artist's egos are. But I was surprised how easy and enriching working with him was. I interpreted his sketches and vice versa. In our first emails we were very respectful about each other's drawings, but finally we broke the respect and I think the results are wonderful.

Now I know that drawing saved me from being a glutton and being devoured by gluttony in my hometown.

And now I know how to work on the same drawing with another guy so far away. This collaboration showed me another way to enjoy drawing.

Zeloot
& Henrik Drescher
on *Fragile*

Zeloot

What does fragile mean to you?
What it means to me is captured in my drawings. I don't like to try to put it in words, they would narrow people's view.

Did working with your collaborator change your view on the theme?
With his work, Henrik made another switch to mine in the second one, I liked that.

How did you find working together?
We didn't really have any conversations about it.

Did you learn something about yourself?
No.

Will this affect your future work?
Who knows...

Henrik Drescher
The final work was really just somethng that we came to individually, we didn't communicate much verbally. I sent her the initial picture, she responded with the two red ink images of what seemed like pustule-covered characters. I was listening to a radio show about viral research, and on it they mentioned the fact that humans are comprised of 10 trillion cells, but that these cells are outnumbered by the approximately 100 trillion bacteria and 4 trillion viruses in our body at any one time. It seemed like an appropriate caption to our pictures, so I used it.

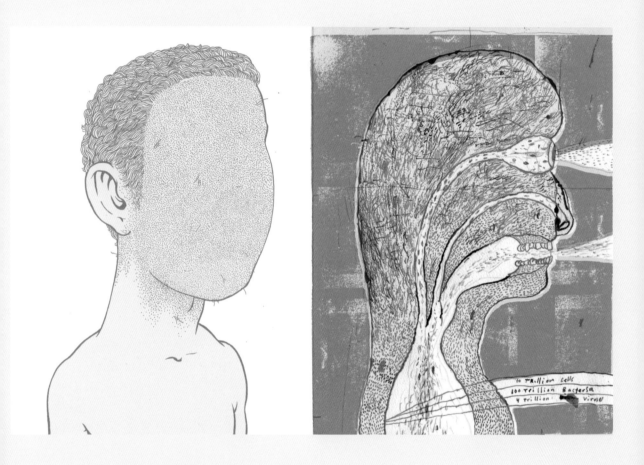

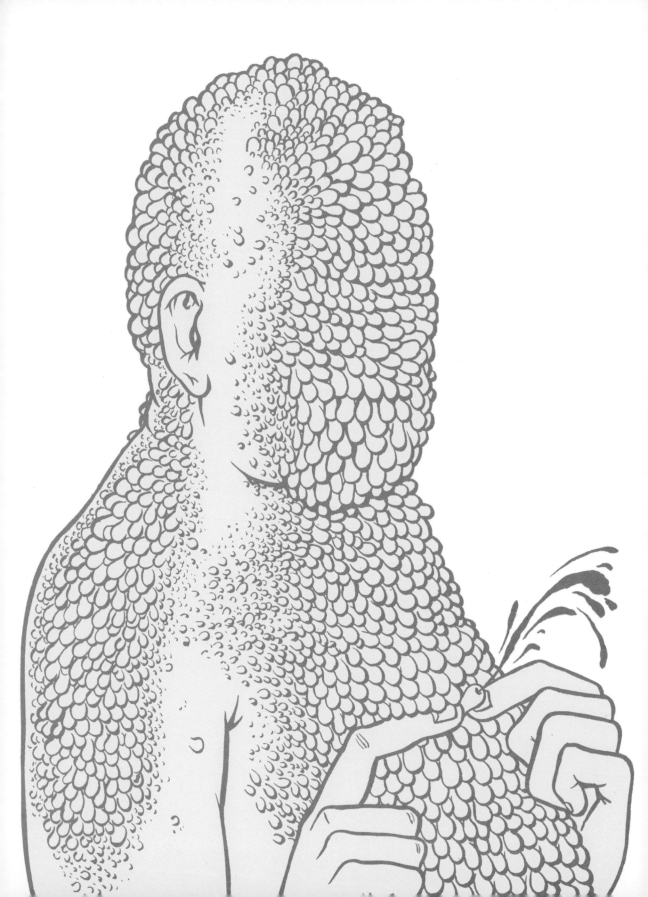

FRA
ȝiLE

Shoboshobo & Yu Matsuoka on *Love*

What does love mean to you?

Shoboshobo: Love is physical, love is psychological – it's hard to define. It's never the same and is still always the same, it happens when you don't expect it to happen and sometimes not when it's supposed to be there.

Yu Matsuoka: I think love is something that is abstract, which can change every moment. I wanted to draw some fragments of love by drawing some objects.

Did working with your collaborator change your view on the theme?

S: I've always considered Yu as someone special to me. We don't see each other that often, but I feel a strong bond between us. Even though our artistic approach is pretty different, it's always really easy for us to match when we work together.

YM: I felt something familial with Mehdi probably because he is a good papa to his son and also I really can count on him in our friendship. I call him my big brother. We tried to make the drawings like love letters and it was fun to do.

How did you find working together? Describe your process and conversations.

S: I've been drawing along with Yu for years now and I cherish those moments. Drawing together is creating a special link between two people which can't be described in words. We don't usually plan to draw something specifically and shapes just appear under our hands while we discuss anything, while drinking tea and smoking together.

YM: I've always loved to work with Mehdi. We collaborated from time to time eating snacks and drawing together. I love to draw with him, to see the lines that I couldn't make if I was drawing alone. It made me discover the freedom of drawing. We worked in Mehdi's atelier and also sent the drawings as letters to make them more like love letters.

Did you learn something about yourself?

S: You always learn something by working with others. I learnt to respect the error and the lack of balance in my own drawings.

YM: I found myself being scared of the lines that I make.

Will this affect your future work?

S: I was really interested in this collaboration, and I hope we can do a whole book together if ever a publisher is interested.

YM: I think so, it's always interesting to see the same thing from many different sides and to collaborate with someone I really trust always makes me feel good and happy. And also it gives me the energy for new creations.

Edel Rodriguez & Drew Beckmeyer on *Heaven*

What does heaven mean to you?

Edel Rodriguez: The concept of heaven is a difficult one for me to work with because I'm not sure heaven exists in any form. For all I know, death could just happen and that's it, the end. Some might think that's morbid, but I guess if something were to exist it would be a pleasant surprise.

Drew Beckmeyer: I was raised really religiously, so the concrete Christian idea of heaven was something that I became very intimate with. Most of my work has to do with faith, losing faith, and trying to find something that fills that hole when you lose faith. Heaven (and I don't subscribe to calling the good moments in life, "heaven"), now, feels like a childish thought...and though I do hope there is some sort of afterlife, I would have to assume that it is something beyond human comprehension and existence, which is a great thought because I'm sorta done with human comprehension.

Did working with your collaborator change your view on the theme?

ER: I went into the image still thinking in somewhat abstract terms – space, light colors, an ethereal kind of place. Drew added more of a real world setting and created a space, so that was a nice surprise – the idea that heaven could be a more realistic, livable space.

DB: Not really. I think Edel has a much more laissez-faire point of view on the theme, which is probably a lot healthier. I've spent some years in semi-crippling states of exhaustion based on worry about if I'll go somewhere when I die, or if I even want to. I mean, it would be hard for me to change my point of view at this point. It would be especially hard for a painting to get me off this precipice.

How did you find working together? Describe your process and conversations.

ER: We live on separate coasts so working together was a bit difficult. In the end, we decided that one would start the piece and the other would finish it. Whoever started first would create the basis of the image. I had a free afternoon and started working on the idea of a kissing couple. The place where one's mind goes to when kissing is kind of heavenly, you forget everything else and sort of float. I finished off the basic structure, left a lot of empty areas around and mailed it off to Drew. I told him he could do whatever he wanted with it, change the image, cover parts, whatever he felt he wanted to do. I saw the final piece a couple of weeks later and was happy to see how he had expanded on the theme, how he had added more space and dimension.

DB: Edel was great to work with. He sent me this really beautiful, elegant, graphic, simple painting and collage. I didn't want to touch it because I'm a bit of a bull in a china shop when it comes to elegance. I spent a few days thinking about how to work on it, without diminishing it, and I decided to give these two abstracted characters he had done a setting in which to be doing what they are doing.

Did you learn something about yourself?

ER: I liked the environment and details that my collaborator added to the image. I tend to work on graphically simple images myself, so the idea of creating complex spaces is something I learned.

DB: I don't think I really learned much about myself through the process. In terms of results, I think this is probably one of the best collaborative pieces I've worked on. Usually, they sort of feel like exercises that really have no personal relevance in terms of subject matter or outside relevance in terms of making an interesting piece. I think this succeeded on both levels, and maybe I should try doing some more work with other people.

Will this affect your future work?

ER: I've collaborated with artists in the past, so the process was similar. The concept of collaboration and letting go is somewhat built into my work already. I would like to do this more often with other artist friends. I think everyone can learn something from the process.

DB: Probably not. I was lucky to get a theme that I've been thinking about my entire life. It fitted right in, but it didn't change a whole lot.

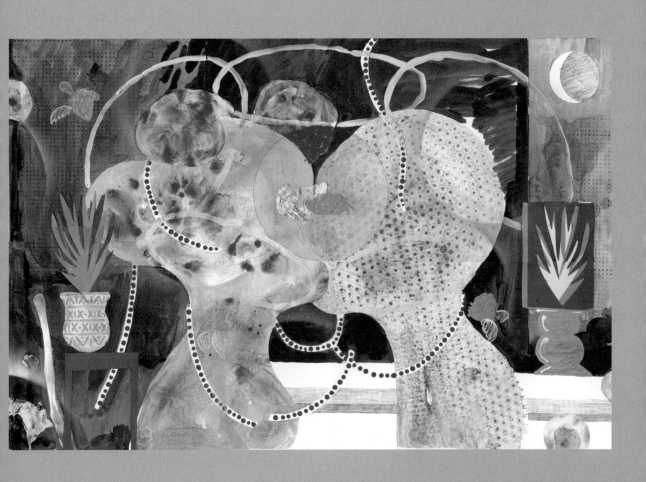

Ahu Sulker & Yuko Shimizu on *Temptation*

What does temptation mean to you?

Ahu Sulker: It's a delicately scattered dream of some sorts. Emphasizing lost thoughts that are uncontrollable and hard to temper. The feeling of losing yourself in your own temptations. A selfless act of agony and loss in your heart. The linework becomes so complicated and intricate that it makes you feel helpless as to where it will end.

Yuko Shimizu: For both of the images, my collaborator did her parts first, so I went with her concepts and enhanced the idea. I didn't really come up with my own interpretation of the theme. So, speaking just about the theme itself in general, temptation is everywhere and it is just a part of life. I always get tempted to eat one more piece of good milk chocolate when I shouldn't. And whenever I start focusing on my drawing, I get an urge to check my email or Facebook…

Did working with your collaborator change your view on the theme?

AS: Yes, I felt that Yuko expressed a rather opposite conclusion to my madness in linework and subject. She re-routed the illustration so it had a simpler design. She expressed openness and emptiness…tempting my ideas which were so intricate. Yuko also allowed my subject to shine and to be expressed by not competing with my linework and scattered marks.

YS: Not really. It may have been different if I had initiated one of them.

How did you find working together? Describe your process and conversations.

AS: I found it very interesting and useful. I was glad we actually did a piece together rather than each person making one page. I started the two layouts and Yuko reacted to them. It was a very simple process and we balanced each other out.

YS: Surprisingly smooth. I don't generally like collaboration. I am a loner. I spent too long working in the corporate world, and that made me allergic to working on something with someone else. Of course, every illustration job is somewhat collaborative in terms of working in harmony with a client, but that is still a lot different from working on a piece of artwork with someone else. I had been going through one of the busiest times in my career for the last however many months, so I had to ask my collaborator to start on them and send them to me so I could finish them whenever I could find extra time. I actually sat with the first image for a long time, trying to figure out what to do. In the end, I decided to "enhance" the work she had started rather than putting my own mark on it. I even changed my regular medium (usually brush and ink on rough paper) to thin nib and ink on a very smooth surface so the lines I made would merge well with the lines she had made. I didn't draw any main objects or figures in the images either, just things to add and complete the drawing. At the end of the day, it is about the final result, and not about the fighting of two styles.

Did you learn something about yourself?

AS: I learned that I lost myself in my linework and the subject more than I thought I would. It opened doors to new ideas with other personal and professional work.

YS: I don't think I necessarily learned anything new about myself, but it was a nice learning process – about how to respect the work that is already on the paper.

Will this affect your future work?

AS: Yes, I believe I found different ways to express my linework and I started to play around with watercolor backgrounds more than I have done in the past.

YS: I will just go back to enjoying being a loner again. Ha ha ha.

MARINA KHARKOVER

Who are you? First I am a self-proclaimed dreamer, for better or for worse. I am always trying to escape the inevitable reality and the practical world. There is just something very morbid and banal about day-to-day life and the only way to remedy that is always to be conspiring creatively. Secondly, I am an idealist. I think that I still hold on to a perhaps naive notion that everything has the potential to be perfect and unblemished. Thirdly, I am a walking contradiction: I disagree with myself about all of the above constantly and to be quite honest the only thing I have really figured out in life thus far is what type of movies and TV shows I like. The rest of me is still a work in progress.

What is your biggest temptation? My biggest temptation is freedom, which is still somewhat of an illusive concept. I often wonder if it will bring me happiness or some kind of peace of mind, or if it is in fact a dangerous and self-destructive force.

Why are things the way they are? Things are the way they are because humankind refuses to let go of the comfortable, conventional and normal. Also because the gender roles are still clearly defined and separated in this society which is still largely governed by the cavemen-like primitive notions of gender specificities. Essentially, we are slaves to our bodies and their so-called "natural functions" and assigned performances.

Where do you find peace? I find peace when I am alone. I think it is important to have time to think things over privately; the world is such a fast place and sometimes it is nice just to think slowly.

When will you be happy? I don't think that I will ever be happy so it is not a question of when. However, I do feel most happy during an epiphany of any sort. When things come together and click in my head I find that moment truly euphoric and equally rare.

How do you know when to stop? I don't know when to stop.

ABOVE LEFT: **Riddle Me This**, personal work, digital, 2010
ABOVE RIGHT: **Aves Cerberus**, personal work, watercolor, 2008
OPPOSITE: **Senshi**, personal work, mixed media, 2011

OPPOSITE: **Spike City**, personal work, digital, 2010
ABOVE LEFT: **Feline Cyclops**, personal work, collage, 2010
ABOVE RIGHT: **Razor Jaws**, personal work, collage, 2010

PAUL LOUBET

Who are you? I'm Paul, born 1987, France.
I actually live in Argentina.

What is your biggest temptation? Chorizo
from the south of France (it's better if it's from
the mountains).
Belgium beer.
Brandade de Morue.
Magrets de canard à l'orange.
Well, most food. I'm not big, I swear.

Why are things the way they are? Why do
you ask me that?

Where do you find peace? Looking at sunsets,
walking on the beach on a rainy day, two
seagulls screaming in the sky. No, sorry, just
drinking with friends.

When will you be happy? I'm happy now.

How do you know when to stop? When
a friend calls me for a beer.

ABOVE LEFT: "Du pain sur la planche,"
personal work, A4, paint on cardboard
ABOVE RIGHT: **Untitled**, A4, thorn paper on
black paper, 2010
OPPOSITE: **Die Ostalgia**, personal work,
paint, 2009

OPPOSITE: **La Baston c'est chic, c'est choc**, silkscreen, *French Fourch*, 2012

RIGHT: **Untitled**, personal work, paint on wood, 24 × 12" (60 × 30 cm), 2011

JUNGYEON
ROH

Who are you? Illustrator, printmaker, sister, daughter, friend, young Korean woman living in New York, not picky vegan, dream of a yogi, runner, someone's ex.

What is your biggest temptation? Something that makes me laugh out loud and delicious food. Harold & Kumar.

Why are things the way they are? Everything has its roles, reasons, and responsibilities because of fate.

Where do you find peace? At a yoga studio, in a shower room, a bedroom, a sauna, a swimming pool, Central Park, a print shop, an organic food market, a Korean restaurant, and at JFK.

When will you be happy? When I have endless hopes and dreams.

How do you know when to stop? I don't know...I've never stopped and I never will!

Desire Series, School of Visual Arts, New York, silkscreen, 2009

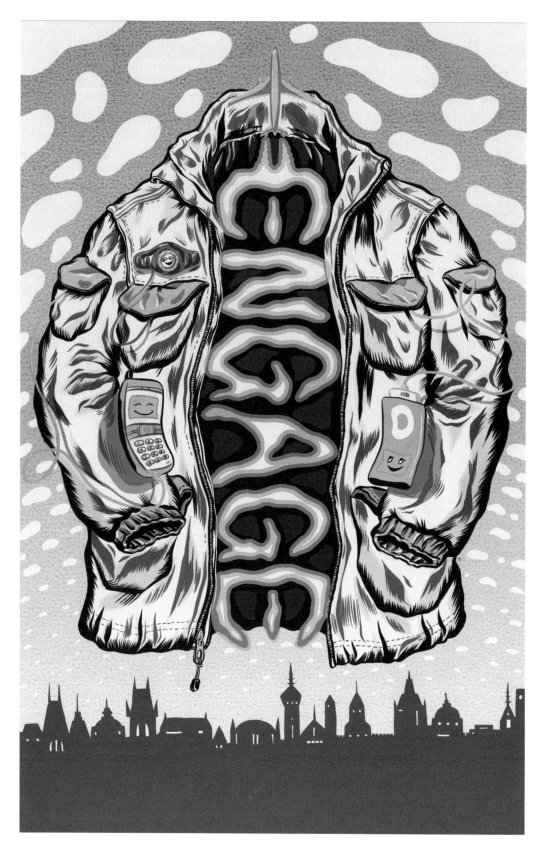

144

OPPOSITE: **Cleveland State University Poster**, Cleveland State
University, Flourish Inc., digital, 2011
ABOVE: **Today is Sushi Day**, School of Visual Arts, New York,
silkscreen, 2008
OVERLEAF: **Today is Sushi Day**, School of Visual Arts, New York,
silkscreen, 2008

ANA ALBERO

Who are you? My name is Ana Albero. I was born and grew up in Alicante, Spain, where I attended a legendary French school. I studied Visual Communication in Paris and Berlin where I specialized in illustration. Since my graduation from the Berlin University of the Arts, I have worked as a freelance illustrator based in Berlin. As part of my commercial work, I put a lot of energy into Edition Biografiktion which is a small self-publishing project I founded together with my fellow illustrators Till Hafenbrak and Paul Paetzel in 2008.

What is your biggest temptation? My biggest temptation is to ignore my alarm clock in the morning and just keep sleeping, especially in winter.

Why are things the way they are? Things are the way they are, but if for some reason you feel unhappy you should try to change something.

Where do you find peace? Hugging my lovely boyfriend, talking to my family on the phone... lately I am also trying out valerian tablets.

When will you be happy? When I finally take the step to adopt a dog at an animal protection society.

How do you know when to stop? Sometimes working as a freelancer is pretty stressful, specially if your workspace is at home. Lately, I have realized how important it is to know when to stop and disconnect. Weekends should be sacred, not for working or checking emails at all!

Southern Carnival, personal work,
pencil and computer coloring, 2010

OPPOSITE: **Heads,** Edition Biografiktion, pencil and computer coloring, 2011
ABOVE: **Personal work** from the series *The Catcher in the Rye* by
J. D. Salinger, pencil and computer coloring, 2011

CAFE CON LECHE

Who are you? We're a couple of deciduous multicellular organisms which, to survive, have taken the form of different organisms for millions of years. We have been luminiscent underwater fungi, apache dinosaurs, giant redwood trees, and now we are regular humans who go by the names of Roi and Inés.

What is your biggest temptation? Sabotaging open-heart surgery to organize races on top of the vital organs with ants on bicycles.

Why are things the way they are? Because of the ever perpetual movement.

Where do you find peace? Under our bedsheets.

When will you be happy? Now!

How do you know when to stop? When eyes itch and arms start to fall off.

ABOVE: **Cintas Chaca**, crayon on coloring book pages, 2009
OPPOSITE: **Untitled** (various stickers), originals on mixed media, 2008–2012

OPPOSITE: **Mundo de chicle**, ballpoint pen and marker, 2010
ABOVE: **Untitled** (various stickers), originals on mixed media, stickers
laser printed on adhesive paper, 2008–2012

BRECHT VANDENBROUCKE

Who are you? Brecht Vandenbroucke and I draw.

What is your biggest temptation? Leaving everything and everyone I know behind.

Why are things the way they are? Because everyone seems too lazy to change a thing.

Where do you find peace? At home. When I'm drawing.

When will you be happy? When I'm dead: rest.

How do you know when to stop? I never stop. I just keep on going. Nothing is ever done, everything keeps on changing.

ABOVE: **Bouncing Jungle**, personal work, painting, A4, acrylic on carton
OPPOSITE: **Sounds to Learn**, personal work, page 2 of a 4-page story, A4, drawing and computer coloring

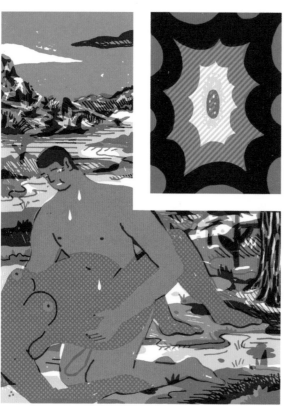

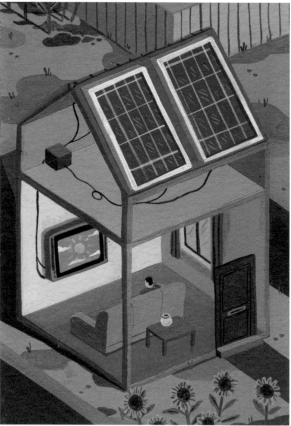

OPPOSITE: **Genesis**, page 4 of a 7-page story for *A Graphic Cosmogony*, A4,
drawing and computer coloring, 2010
ABOVE LEFT: **Last Minute Shopping**, *Humo*, no. 3667, A3, acrylic
on paper, December 14, 2010
ABOVE RIGHT: **Solar Power**, personal work, painting, A4, acrylic on carton

GUSTAVO EANDI

Who are you? Hi, my name is Gustavo Eandi. I'm an artist born in 1981 in Mar del Plata, Argentina. Although working with different techniques and formats, my main commitment is to drawing. It's the basis of all my projects and I practise and study daily.

What is your biggest temptation? I'm very interested in the "subcultures" and their own audio/visual production, mostly generated in an amateur way, far from conventional parameters. Old books of ancient pagan cults, fanzines, posters, and flyers (first rave parties, teenage bands from my town, sexual proposals, etc.) as well as discontinued LPs or those from very short runs (no genre in particular) are part of my file. Rather than "collecting," I am interested in the "file" as a structure, as a genre in itself. I search, buy, and gather with the idea that what I keep will become part of my work.

Where do you find peace? There are situations that I remember, when I was a kid, like when I went to the beach early in the summer, it was great. Maybe these days I do not have a physical place to turn in search of that feeling, but I find similar times on the road, traveling at sunset, bike riding at night or drawing in silence in the early morning.

Why are things the way they are? For me, and more precisely with my work, things are how they are because of effort and maybe by accident. If things go well, fairly badly or just badly, this is because of everything I was influenced by during the creative process. My mood, the music I heard that week, the time I lost, the people I spoke to, the books and magazines I read...

When will you be happy? I think there will not be a time to say: "Well, now yes, from now on I'm happy." But no matter. I can say I'm happy a couple of times a week. The reasons may vary. Sometimes they are related to my work (I spend a lot of the week working) and sometimes the motives are as—or more—important.

How do you know when to stop? I do not know when to stop, actually. I mean, I do not know if when I have stopped it was the "right time," if "a little more" would have been better, or, conversely, "too much (wasteful) work". Implementing this supposed excess (which implies a certain decontrol over the paper) makes it interesting to both the process and the outcome.

ABOVE: **Carne Cruda** (Raw Meat), personal work, synthetic enamel on paper, 2009
OPPOSITE, CLOCKWISE FROM TOP LEFT: **"Guided by Tourists,"** graphite on paper, 14 × 20" (35 × 50 cm), part of a zine commissioned by Landfill Editions (UK), 2011; **Arnau Sala/Oscar Barras: Remixes,** ink on paper, Ozonokids Records (Spain), 2008; **"Guided by Tourists,"** graphite on paper, 14 × 20" (35 × 50 cm), part of a zine commissioned by Landfill Editions (UK), 2011; **"Amigo de Los Grandes,"** personal work, acrylic on paper, 18 × 26" (45 × 65 cm), 2008

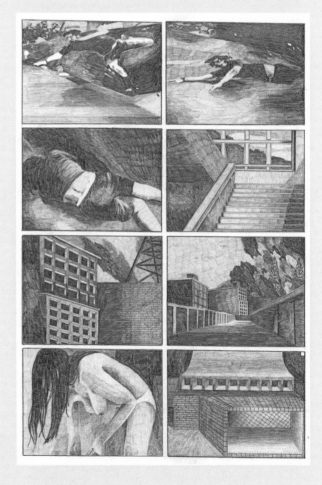

162

OPPOSITE: **"Altar,"** personal work, graphite and collage on paper,
30 × 43" (75 × 110 cm), 2010
ABOVE FROM LEFT TO RIGHT: **"El Fin del Underground,"** #2 ("The End of the
Underground," #2); **"El Fin del Underground,"** #1 ("The End of the
Underground," #1), personal project, photocopy and mixed media, 2011

SIMON ROUSSIN

Who are you? I graduated in illustration from the Ecole supérieure des arts décoratifs in Strasbourg in 2011 and moved to Paris to pursue my work in illustration and comics. I try, by working on the "récit de genre," to find the jubilation I had as a child reading comic books, watching movies, and drawing my first comics in school notebooks. I tell tales of extraordinary adventures, loyal friendship, and lost love!

What is your biggest temptation? I say sometimes, as a joke, that I could quit everything to become an archaeologist and travel the world! I appreciate the solitude, but imagining stories sometimes isolates me a bit too much from the real world. However, there's nothing more exciting for me than to write the words "the end" in a story and get into the unknown of another tale. I'll be Indiana Jones when I have time!

Why are things the way they are? I think that things are not condemned to remain fixed. I try constantly to question myself in order to move forward, take risks rather than remain idle. I try as much as possible to avoid boredom in my work.

Where do you find peace? I am often told that I live in the movies I love and watch over and

over. In times of doubt or trouble, a movie can give me much more comfort than anything else. I can find solutions in them, ideas to explore, a desire to move forward. *Once Upon a Time in America* is my favorite of all time. I must see it every year – nothing surpasses this movie in my mind. But listening to the words of Michel Audiard coming out of the mouths of Lino Ventura, Bernard Blier, or Jean-Paul Belmondo can calm me a lot too!

When will you be happy? Since I was young I have always responded without hesitation to the question, "what do you want to do later?" with "be an author of comic books". Starting to see this childhood dream, little by little, become a reality amazes me already. Besides, I would have been a terrible veterinarian!

How do you know when to stop? As long as I still want to imagine stories, to have the need to try to be critical of my work and the will to do better, I won't think of the end. A project leads to another one. But, obviously, I am very scared to get to the point of being repetitive, exhausted, and not finding anything to say.

ABOVE: **Les Aventuriers**, Editions Magnani, ink on paper and numeric colors, 2012
OPPOSITE: **Lemon Jefferson et la grande aventure**, Editions 2024, ink and felt-tip pen on paper, published November 2011

Le perdant de ce combat finira dans les flammes au sommet du temple. Le vainqueur accèdera à la Caverne des délices.

C'est un lieu secret où toutes les femmes sont réunies. Ainsi, chaque lauréat pourra assurer la descendance de la race humaine.

Les affrontements sont arbitrés par nos deux chefs suprêmes.

Bats-toi, Lemon Jefferson !

Lemon est abasourdi.

Je n'ai aucune raison de me battre ! Et comment connaissez-vous mon nom ?!

Je vais t'en donner une de raison, froussard !

Un enfant ?! Je ne peux combattre un enfant !

YRRRRRRR

ABOVE: **Robin Hood**, L'Employé du moi,
ink and felt-tip pen on paper, 2010
OPPOSITE: **Lemon Jefferson et la grande aventure**, Editions 2024,
ink and felt-tip pen on paper, published November 2011

Lemon Jefferson est désormais le souverain de la Terre.
Il règne en maître sur le monde qui abrita les plus beaux
et les plus tragiques instants de son existence.

Les nuits d'insomnie, se retrouvant seul sous la lune,
il contemple l'immensité de son royaume.

MU PAN

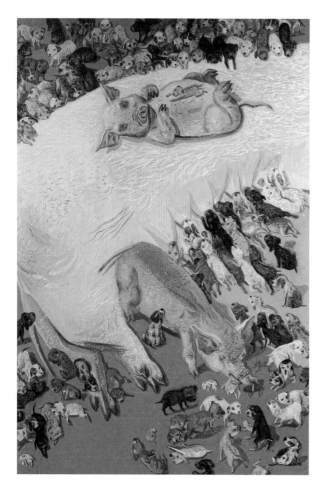 

Who are you? I am Chinese.

What is your biggest temptation?
Watching "Breaking Bad."

Why are things the way they are?
People talk too much here.

Where do you find peace?
Dozing off on the subway.

When will you be happy?
When I've paid off my mortgage.

How do you know when to stop?
When it becomes too much.

ABOVE: **Pig Milk and Dog Piss**, oil, 2010
OPPOSITE: **Heavenly Book of China**,
Chapter 8, watercolor on paper, 2009

宣統皇帝御駕親征臨陣斬妖魔
尚方寶劍洛火九天陣前斬餓鬼

有詩為證：
佛王之命非由己，
國亡朝異月天忽；
主宰神州三世紀，
義終信乘棟於戴。
慢我滿域東三地，
略我嫣跨下騎，
還見我單不爭氣，
在天亡靈方能忽。

敖拜

餓鬼尊者

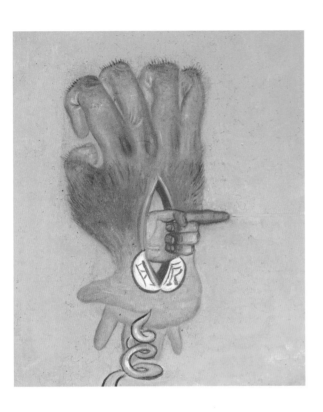

OPPOSITE: **Heavenly Book of China**, chapter 2: the 108 outlaws from the marsh, watercolor on paper, 30 × 40" (76 × 102 cm), 2009
ABOVE LEFT: **Hand Job Series**, oil, 2003
ABOVE RIGHT: **Bruce Lee, the Bad Ass Chinese American**, ballpoint pen, color pencil on paper, 11 × 17" (28 × 43 cm), 2006

RYAN CECIL SMITH

Who are you? Young, an artist, American, still dumb.

What is your biggest temptation? To get home and take a nap even though I have a lot to do. Or watch online videos, or go through hundreds of entries in Google Reader, or anything that will amount to just sitting on my butt in my apartment. I am ashamed to fall to this temptation very often!

Why are things the way they are? Because the Universe is very big, God doesn't exist, and humans are selfish.

Where do you find peace? Peace would be anxiety free, and I never feel that way. I worry a lot about the future and money and where to go, so I look forward to the time when those things are balanced, if not totally figured out.

When will you be happy? I'm very happy when I make something good, or do something right, or I finish something well. I'm also happy when the weather is good and when I see someone I love.

How do you know when to stop? Avoid extremes, try to meet simple goals, find a wider perspective.

ABOVE: **Muscle Camp**, handmade lithograph, edition of 17, 2008
OPPOSITE: **Drawings for** *Picnic at Tough Beach*, brush and ink, self-published, photocopied zine, 2007

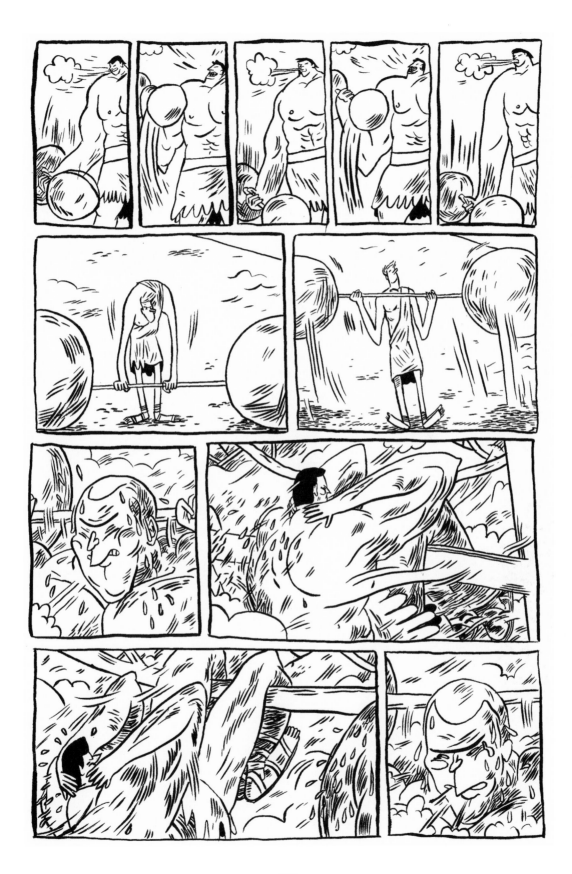

ABOVE: **Cover of WSII**, self-published photocopied zine, 2009
OPPOSITE, FROM TOP CLOCKWISE: **Picnic at Tough Beach (inside cover art)**,
self-published edition of 150-screen-printed and photocopied
32-page book, October 2007; **Misty Morning (cover)**, self-published
edition of 100 risograph printed 12-page book, January 2009; **Two
Eyes of the Beautiful II (cover)**, self-published edition of 250 gocco-
printed and risographed 48-page book, November 2010

IT'S A GROTESQUE HORROR MANGA. IT'S BASED ON UMEZU KAZUO'S "BLOOD BAPTISM" IT'S BY RYAN CECIL SMITH.

TWO EYES OF THE BEAUTIFUL

PART II

MISTY MORNING

DRAWINGS FROM INDIA
= VARANASI, AGRA, GOA + MORE
DEC '08 - JAN '09   RCJ

Marina Kharkover & Paul Loubet on *Age*

What does age mean to you?

Marina Kharkover: My theme was age and to be honest I was initially stumped on how to interpret that. I began thinking about broad concepts such as the passing of time. I also thought about the theme's relevance to me and specifically how society demands that each person act in an "age appropriate way". I find it hard to part with my own youthfulness and descend into perpetual adulthood. I see this transition almost as a thread that separates me from some, while linking me closer to others. More than ever, I feel pressure from my family and friends to establish my identity as a wife and a mother. Things such as the withering of youth and beauty, the biological clock and pair bonding seem to come to the forefront and demand to be noticed. This mounting pressure leads me to cling to a childlike escapist dream of a reality that is permeated with idealist notions and fantastical fairytale-like outcomes. Thus I did not want to create something heavy and burdened by deep philosophical discourse. Instead, I yearned to create a whimsical self-indulgent image that brings the viewer back to the possibility of what if… Essentially, I longed to re-create possibility.

Paul Loubet: It means everything and nothing, but it was a good excuse to draw dinosaurs in sneakers.

Did working with your collaborator change your view on the theme?

MK: Paul Loubet had a tremendous impact on how I viewed the theme of age. He suggested that we steer clear of themes relating to physical age such as young woman/old woman and navigate more towards periods in time. He revealed to me that his two favorite periods in time are the prehistoric age and the medieval age but that he was having a hard time deciding which one he liked more. It just so happens that those are also my two favorite time periods so I suggested that instead of choosing we combine the two. This type of playful collaborative thinking was just what I needed to get the ball rolling. Without much hesitation, my collaborator and I decided on a loose theme of a mesh of time periods and the results were quite delightful.

PL: Possibly. In fact, we started with a very broad overall idea, and we sent each other our work as we went along. So maybe it did change, as things progressed.

How did you find working together? Describe your process and conversations.

MK: Working with my partner was a pleasure. I think that we complemented each other's sensibilities both artistically and intellectually. I really enjoyed his creative input and his outlook on the theme. Initially we both decided that our work would entail both aspects of the prehistoric and medieval time periods and we bounced around ideas that included dragons and knights co-existing with dinosaurs in the fantastical environment. We exchanged inspirational images, so that we could better acquaint ourselves with our likes and dislikes. We also presented some compositional sketches to each other so that we would have a better idea as to how we would divide our mutual compositional space. After some deliberation, Paul and I agreed that it would be best if we each worked on our own two pages since he lives in France and I live in the US. However, we agreed to send each other constant updates regarding our art. The end result for both of us loosely incorporated these time periods and I think that my partner and I transcended our original discourse through modernizing those specific time frames.

PL: Well, after we'd agreed on the overall idea, we sent each other the work as it evolved and some inspirational influences. It was very free.

Did you learn something about yourself?

MK: This collaboration solidified my suspicions that the creative process of making art is my primary form of escapism. For this project I created a fantastical scene that depicts fantastical knights (based on medieval warriors) in an epic battle scene using giant monsters (based on dinosaurs) as their main source of transportation. In this illustration I allowed myself to pay close attention to the details and create an intricate background, which I do not usually do. I also found myself playing with color in a more complex and unexpected way.

PL: I need to improve my English.

Will this affect your future work?

MK: Through this experience I realized that I derive great pleasure in visual story telling, by creating spirited and often irrational narratives. I suspect that this notion will permeate my future work.

PL: Yes. I'm much better at drawing dinosaurs.

Jungyeon Roh & Ana Albero on *Farm*

What does farm mean to you?

Jungyeon Roh: My theme was farm and I drew "A hen who laid golden eggs on a farm" to make good fortune.

Ana Albero: For me, farm means drawing lots of animals. I have done a couple of farm drawings before, but this time I wanted to show the interior of a farm and not the usual animal farm scenery.

Did working with your collaborator change your view on the theme?

JR: No, but I changed colors, depending on what my partner used.

AA: Yes, I changed my former idea after seeing Jungyeon's first sketch.

How did you find working together?

JR: I drew first, and Ana got the idea of having "A hen who laid golden eggs" in her drawing. She then colored first and I used the same color palettes.

AA: I started to sketch an old farm interior...but after seeing Jungyeon's approach I felt that our drawings should be more connected so I changed my scene. My final drawing shows a farmer lady who has just found a golden egg laid by one of the hens, which relates to Jungyeon's idea of "A hen who laid golden eggs on a farm".

Did you learn something about yourself?

JR: I want to be the hen who laid golden eggs in America.

AA: That I am very lazy about answering emails (well, that's nothing new).

Will this affect your future work?

JR: I had lots of fun doing a collaboration with Ana Albero – her work motivated me a lot.

AA: It would be great to work for US clients more often. I hope this book reaches a large audience.

Café con Leche & Brecht Vandenbroucke on *Death*

What does death mean to you?

Café con Leche: We cannot arrive at a consensus about the answer to this question, more than that it is an uncertain state.

Brecht Vandenbroucke: Death is something that I think about daily, so I was happy with the theme. Life is short, so I see knowing we're all going to die as a constant motivator to search for personal freedom and to work hard. There is no time for fear and there will never be enough time to do everything you want.

Did working with your collaborator change your view on the theme?

CCL: No, because we never talked with Brecht about the subject, only about how to work on the process. Besides, we consider that neither of us had the intention of expressing a stance in our representation of the theme.

BV: Not really, but that's not a bad thing.

How did you find working together?

CCL: We agreed on doing half of each spread so the other one would complete the remaining part. We had a bit of confusion in the making of this, but we enjoyed working on it and loved the result anyway.

BV: At first I was a bit hesitant because it's difficult to merge two personal worlds or visions... That's why I don't really like collaborations as they always lead to compromises. I don't like compromises, I like everyone's work to be in full force. But I think we found a good way. I made the first drawing, they made the second and so on. They somehow respond in a stream of consciousness way that maybe no one else will understand.

Did you learn something about yourself?

CCL: We hadn't worked on something serious with a pre-established subject in a long time, we generally just draw without any previous idea, so it was nice realizing we're able to do it, and still have fun in the meantime. It's funny that the few times we've had to work on specific themes, most of them have been about death!

BV: Maybe that I should reply faster to emails.

Will this affect your future work?

CCL: We want to paint more with our feet in future pieces, it was very gratifying and gave delightful results.

BV: We'll have to see, I guess!! :-)

Gustavo Eandi & Simon Roussin on *Me*

What does me mean to you?

Gustavo Eandi: It is a very straightforward theme, even uncomfortable – if you are a bit susceptible. I tried to take it as non-personal, talking about me but in a fictional and funny/silly way, which is how I usually work.

Simon Roussin: Talking about yourself is always very difficult. I'm not the kind of person who likes to do that, so I decided to treat this subject in such a way that I could talk about myself but not openly. The cinema has an important place in my daily life. I often watch scenes that I love again and again, the same movie several times, and I read stories about shootings, and actors' or directors' biographies. So, starting from the scene in *Manhattan* in which Woody Allen enumerates what makes life worthwhile to his mind, I chose to make a modest, not exhaustive and completely subjective list of memories of movies that make life worthwhile!

Did working with your collaborator change your view on the theme?

GE: No, I was open to Simon's proposals from the beginning, but my vision of myself does not change with a comic, ha!

SR: First I thought it would be impossible to talk about such a specific and personal theme as me with someone that I don't know and whose work is far from mine. But it's a good challenge, and it forced me to work differently, to break the habit in a very exciting way.

How did you find working together?

GE: I designed the sizes of the vignettes and who drew on each. I started with the first frame on page one. That was the kick. Then Simon did what he wanted!

SR: Initially, we established a pattern and divided the pages in an equitable way. We wanted to mix our works, we thought it would be more interesting than dividing the four

pages into two distinct parts. I had the idea of using moments of films that I love and I submitted this idea to Gustavo. Whatever he did in response, our works would meet and mix in an original way. We also wanted to leave the project to chance, to let ourselves be surprised by the result. Gustavo sent me his first picture. I sent him mine and then the rest of my contribution. We exchanged our impressions by mail and then he sent me his final work.

Did you learn something about yourself?

GE: It is hard to work with someone you do not know.

SR: It was very pleasant to work on this topic because I always wanted to do a project about my great interest in movies, actors I idolized in my childhood and I still admire today, but I never found a form that suited me perfectly. Finally, I took great pleasure in drawing these scenes, these great actors and great lines and transcribing them using a felt-tip pen.

Will this affect your future work?

GE: I took up the use of color. That was good for me. I'll continue.

SR: Working from screenshots, drawing actors whose faces are known to all, forced me to change my line a little. I wanted to keep my clumsiness but approach it in a style that was a little bit more realist. My line became a bit more precise, the black and shadows more present. Also, I tried to use the felt-tip pen in a different way than I usually do in my comics. I was so pleased to be drawing these scenes that I decided to continue this project. I had a book of anecdotes, actors, memorable scenes or quotes that have stuck in my mind, so I drew them. I'd like to do much more than a hundred of these, and perhaps make a book with them. A book of references and memories of films that you can open anywhere, dig in, and find some familiar faces – beautiful dialogues that can resonate in your head. It's still the beginning, but who knows?

A Truckload OF TROUBLES.

Well, all right. Why is life worth living? That's a very good question...

Well, there are certain things, I guess, that make it...

Worthwhile

SIMON ROUSSIN

Dean Martin and Ricky Nelson singing in RIO BRAVO.

Purple light in the canyon That's where I long to be ...

Gene Kelly tap dancing on roller skates in IT'S ALWAYS FAIR WEATHER.

Interlude

Steve McQueen, Jean-Louis Trintignant, a voice, Delphine Seyrig in BAISERS VOLÉS, James Coburn, Lino Ventura, Paul Newman and Robert Redford in BUTCH CASSIDY AND THE SUNDANCE KID, Jean-Pierre Cassel, Robert Ryan, Cary Grant, James Stewart, Paul Meurisse, Martin Sheen and Sissy Spacek dancing in the night on a Nat King Cole song in BADLANDS, absolutely everything from ONCE UPON A TIME IN AMERICA, Karen Steele in RIDE LONESOME, Jean-Paul Belmondo, Michael Constantin, Angie Dickinson in RIO BRAVO, Patrick Dewaere, Schubert's impromptu in G flat major, op. 90 D. 899 in TROP BELLE POUR TOI, Marilyn Monroe singing RIVER OF NO RETURN, Robert Mitchum, Jason Robards, ... singing COLOURS ... Melville

Jean Seberg's hair.

Tu es si belle. Quand je te regarde, c'est une souffrance.

Pourtant, hier tu disais que c'était une joie.

... C'est une joie et une souffrance.

The snow at the end of LA SIRÈNE DU MISSISSIPPI.

This shot from PAT GARRETT AND BILLY THE KID.

gettin' dark, too dark to see. I feel I'm kn...

UK DUK DUK DUK DUK DUK

Nena Nena, no me llores

The words of François Truffaut in *LA NUIT AMÉRICAINE*.

Les films sont plus harmonieux que la vie, Alphonse. Il n'y a pas d'embouteillages dans les films, il n'y a pas de temps morts.

Les films avancent comme des trains, tu comprends ? Comme des trains dans la nuit...

Some sex scenes were deleted by the Author.

The voice-over in *THE LADY FROM SHANGAÏ*.

Maybe I'll live so long that I'll forget her. Maybe I'll die trying.

The End

Mu Pan &
Ryan Cecil Smith
on *Body*

What does body mean to you?

Mu Pan: Nothing particular.

Ryan Cecil Smith: My body isn't "who I am," but it's automatically a part of me and it's with me all the time. I use it for everything, but it's also kind of an ever-present limitation for me.

Did working with your collaborator change your view on the theme?

MP: No.

RCS: I liked his phrase, "This is my body, this is my best body."

How did you find working together?

MP: We went on our own.

RCS: We started by sharing some information about ourselves as well as the answers to the first set of questions.

We both like to communicate pretty directly. We learned that neither of us are used to working with collaborators. I started with the idea that we would participate in each other's work, but actually we really worked independently after our very first conversations.

Did you learn something about yourself?

MP: No.

RCS: Not so much!

Will this affect your future work?

MP: No.

RCS: This was more directly introspective than anything else I do. Even though I'm speaking "through" some characters in a little "story," the words are a conversation in my head. I liked doing it, but I can't say if I'll do something like this again soon.

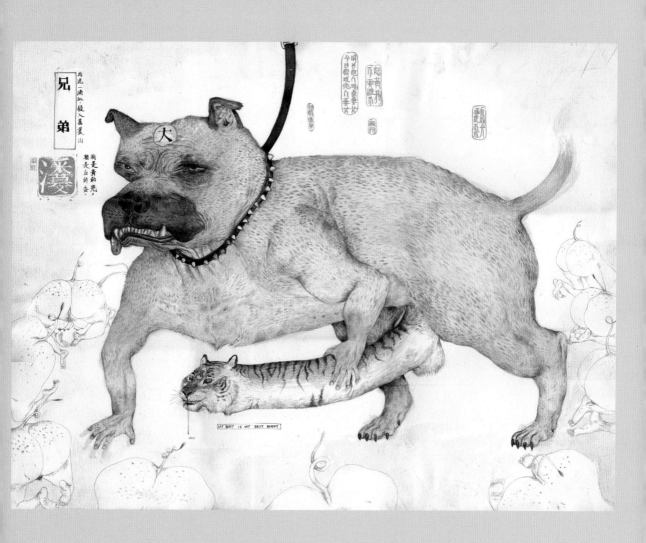

DANIEL KRALL

Who are you? I started out in a wide open space and then elected to move around inside lots of smaller ones instead. I make drawings, tell stories, and discuss other people's drawings and stories for a living. I'm the sum of my experiences and I've been lucky enough to have had a lot of unique ones. I'm not particularly materialistic, yet I seem to accumulate bunches of stuff. I'm the son of two kind and generous people who were a lot more practical about their choices than I've been. I'm a procrastinator and a lover of long conversations, though I readily switch gears into solitary work-horse mode. I think of what I do as a professional form of lying, but I figure it's generally pretty beneficial as a jumping-off point for people's imaginations. I'm Daniel Krall, one of roughly seven billion terrifying hairless apes cruising around their respective continents trying to do something cool, and hitting the mark every once in a while.

What is your biggest temptation? I have lots of temptations that are kind of aspirational, so I'm not sure they count for a question like this. Other ones are crazy, spur-of-the-moment things like walloping someone or eating the most pie ever. Sometimes I think about leaving. I'm sure lots of people do, so it's not an especially peculiar feeling. I think about packing up in the dead of night and just disappearing in that romantic way people do in movies. Very mysterious. See, the problem with that is that I'm not particularly good at anything besides what I already do. I'd either have to go back to school to study something else or change my name and start my illustration career over again. Eventually someone would be like: "Hey, Clayton Vanderbunce draws an awful lot like Daniel Krall" and I'd have to say something like: "What, that hack? He hasn't done anything in years." Then I'd have to come out of the woodwork and retaliate. It'd be a mess.

Why are things the way they are? Because people are really good at convincing us they should be this way. I'm pretty sure we like the things we like because someone made a really persuasive argument. I mean, there are basic things like something tastes good to you so you eat it. That's maybe a higher mystery connected to collective consciousness or something. The desire we have for the things we enjoy or feel like we need to see or own are the direct result of a chain of influence. That sometimes leads to lots of good stuff, though. As far as the badness? I figure it all boils down to an even combination of fear, greed, and laziness. The most immediate problem we're getting smacked with is the breakdown of social interaction, a mild stagnation of creativity in large popular venues, and the gradual cultivation of a weird relationship with learning. I blame the current relationship we have with the internet. If you spend the bulk of your time drifting in a void of questionable information barking about what you're thinking I feel like you end up learning very little and living in a sad bubble. We learn by searching for and experiencing things. By having face-to-face conversations with people who sometimes disagree with us. When you search for things in the real world you come by them in unexpected ways and remember them by way of the journey you took to reach them. I feel like our memories are the fuel for our imagination, and imagination breeds ingenuity and invention. If you keep spinning around in the same circles, being exposed to the same things, it spreads like wildfire and everything ends up at this weird nebulous middle ground. Things aren't phenomenally better or worse than they've ever been. People are weird, though, and now some of them are creepier in person than they might have been otherwise.

Where do you find peace? At the movies, and then at dinner after the movies. I'd like to say that it's during some kind of awesome inspired moment of divine creativity, but I'm usually churning pretty hard when I'm drawing something. I've always liked going to a theater to see a movie. Some of my very best memories

OPPOSITE: **Paul and Linda McCartney**, unpublished, 2009

are associated with films. The movies I saw as a kid heavily influenced my approach to narrative in my work. Whether it's editorial work or a sequential piece of some sort, I usually start with a simple story and build from there.

When will you be happy? I don't know. I think it's important never to be completely satisfied professionally (but not to the point where it's crippling). I think I'd be pretty happy if I managed to come up with a story that sticks with people. If I ever saw a kid pretending to be a character I came up with...that would make me pretty happy, I think. I really like stories and the telling of stories. I've read, watched, and listened to so many good ones over the years. It really makes me want to contribute something of my own.

How do you know when to stop? Well, if that's the big "when to stop," then never. Never ever ever. If it's the smaller project by project "when to stop" I think it's much easier. I get a picture in my head of what I want something to look or feel like. Then I attack it to the best of my ability. When I feel like I've exhausted my ability and I've gotten as close as my clumsy meat paws will allow to the picture in my head I call it quits and move on to avoid obsessive tweaking and self-loathing. I try to know when to say when, build the art muscles some more, and then approach the next project knowing a little more than I did the last time. I don't figure I'll ever reach that "picture in my head," but maybe when I'm a very old Daniel Krall I'll get kinda close.

RIGHT: *McSweeney's Lucky Peach* magazine, 2011. "The article, 'Instant Ramen Showdown,' was created for a gallery show in Baltimore called 'Black Metal Fast Food Fight' in 2008. It is otherwise unpublished. It's the Wendy's girl summoning a hamburger demon. Kind of ridiculous."
OPPOSITE: "This was for an article in the *Baltimore City Paper* entitled 'Zipper Ripper' published in 2009. It was about sexy romantic fiction centered around gay men but written for heterosexual female readers, and how that's a seriously growing genre."

JEONG HWA MIN

Who are you? I am Jeong Hwa Min and I was born in Busan, South Korea. Since 2006 I have been living and working as an illustrator in Berlin. I am currently studying illustration at the University of the Arts, Berlin. I am a cat lover, a heavy smoker, and a curious observer of the people and the world around me.

What is your biggest temptation? All beautiful illustrations and books where images and stories are a surprising interaction. I was a kid who read books all the time, who liked the smell of books and slept with books. I think that since my childhood I have wanted to draw and make stories – because it was the thing that made me most happy. I know when people read books with inspiring images and stories they are having an extraordinary experience which exists solely in the books. I want to create these kind of books on my own account. Somehow I feel like this is the only thing that I can do and and that makes me happy.

Why are things the way they are? Who knows? I think that the world is full of problems which are already acknowledged but not solved, such as isolation in city life, miscommunications, unequal distributions, and wars. Rather than wanting to believe in blind optimism, I focus on toughly enduring life as it is.

Where do you find peace? In my warm workroom during the cold Berlin winter, equipped with a neat drawing desk, a desk lamp, organized colors, a clean triangle ruler, well-sharpened pencils, and blank paper.

When will you be happy? I am happy about my daily routine which I've been trying to set up during the past few years: I can think and work on drawings all the time while I'm awake. This kind of concentrated everyday life makes me feel quite fulfilled. And I can picture myself going on like this.

How do you know when to stop? Shortly before the excess.

ABOVE: **Dive into Blossom**, personal work, ink and digital coloring, 2011
OPPOSITE: **Two Doors, Future Pforte**, pencil and ink, 2012

ABOVE: **Reisen nach Israel**, personal work,
pencil and digital coloring, 2010

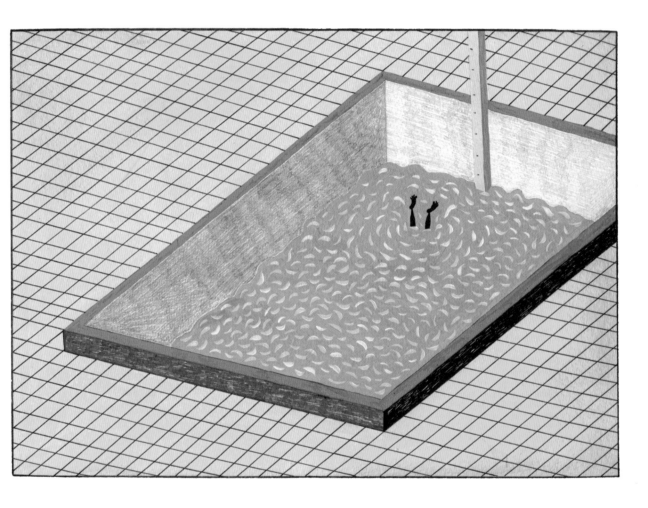

ABOVE: **Swimming Pool**, personal work,
pencil and acrylic, 2011

SOPHY HOLLINGTON

Who are you? My name is Sophy Hollington.
I just graduated from studying illustration at
Camberwell College of Arts in London and have
been living here, drawing and stuff, since then.
I like tailfins, doomsday theories, Jim Shepherd,
and terriers.

What is your biggest temptation? Jumping
on that plane to Hawaii and never coming back.

Why are things the way they are?
I think it's a combination of chronic laziness,
compulsive mark-making, germs, and fire.

Where do you find peace? When I'm at my
most productive. I guess that's when I can stop
worrying about not being productive which is
all I worry about really, that and asteroids.

When will you be happy? When I'm being
hugely productive and living in Hawaii.

How do you know when to stop? I hold
my drawings up to a mirror or look at them
upside down.

ABOVE: **Party Beyond**, pen, pencil,
and Photoshop, 2011
OPPOSITE: **Lily**, pen, pencil, and
Photoshop, 2011

ABOVE: **Perfect Chicken**, pen, pencil, and Photoshop. 2011
OPPOSITE: **Work, Work, Work,** The *New York Times Sunday Review*
cover, linocut, 2011

KYLE PLATTS

Who are you? I am an illustrator and designer born in Sheffield living in London. I recently graduated from Camberwell College of Arts in London, and I am now working freelance. Most of my work uses humour, I like to satirize and make light of the sinister. I also love to write and illustrate comics, of which the content is usually quite crude.

What is your biggest temptation? I am tempted to shell out for a rented studio, I love the idea of having a space where I can make large paintings or sculptures if I feel like it. I am also forever tempted to buy an Xbox. I am holding myself back—if I had one my career would almost certainly be over. I get overexcited when I go to a friend's house and they have "Call of Duty".

Why are things the way they are? Well, that's a very long story, but it's probably got something to do with the basic laws of physics

and a few other things. I know that my kitchen is in a complete state at the moment because someone decided to steel my wheelie bin, the rubbish is just piling up. I should probably call the council for a new one.

Where do you find peace? I find peace when I am drawing, I have the radio on with my favorite programs and I have a cup of tea and a bunch of snacks. That kind of puts me in a Zen-like state. I also enjoy running, it's a total cliché, but I do feel pretty calm when I am out running.

When will you be happy? I will be chuffed when my book *Megaskull* gets published by Nobrow later this year. It will be my first published comic book, I'm so excited! Also, I feel like my life as an illustrator will be much better/more secure/more consistent once I have got an agent.

ABOVE LEFT: **Smoking for Two**, personal work, rotring pen, 2011
ABOVE RIGHT: **Frontier Man**, personal work, medium rotring pen, 2012
OPPOSITE: **Go Old**, Clinic Presents, rotring pen, 2011

OPPOSITE: **High Five, High Five**, brush pen, 2011
ABOVE: **Robot Doppelganger**, Nobrow, rotring pen,
lithograph print, 2011

ADRIANA LOZANO

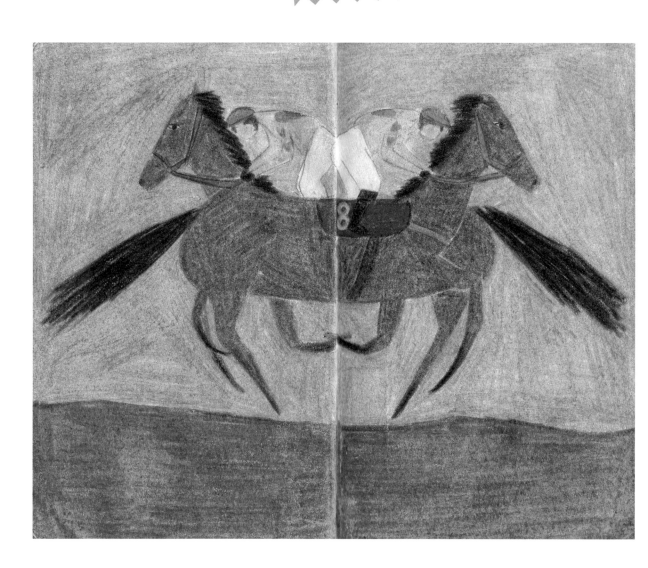

Who are you? A human being.

What is your biggest temptation?
Bad wishes, good wishes.

Why are things the way they are?
Because if things were different we would ask
the same question anyway.

Where do you find peace? When I lose, then
I find (to infinity and beyond).

When will you be happy? Piña colada.

How do you know when to stop? The world
turns faster than I do.

ABOVE: **No, apuesta ganada**, personal
work, 2011
OPPOSITE CLOCKWISE, FROM TOP LEFT: **Self-
portrait**, personal work, 2011; **Pelea
fantasma**, personal work, 2011;
**Libélula mecánica gigante con cabeza
hueca y lámpara de restaurante**,
personal work, 2011

Bellagamba, personal work, 2011

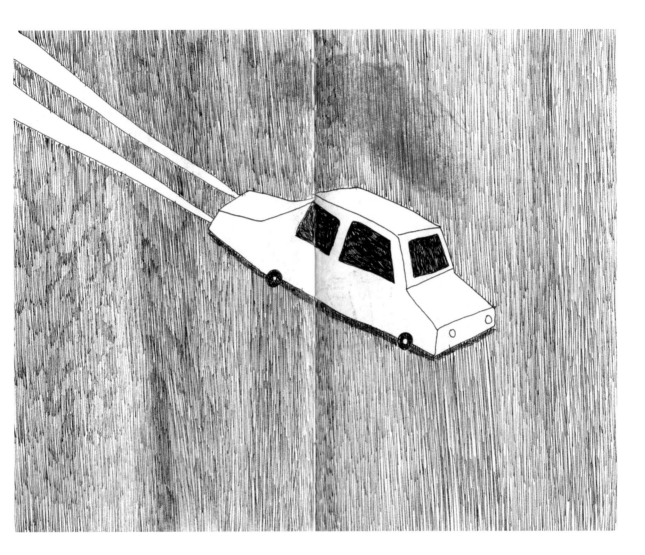

Carro angelito, personal work, 2011

WENG PIXIN

Who are you? My name is Pixin. Memories and desires are sources of inspiration for my drawings and comics.

What is your biggest temptation? To see bullies get run over by a stampede of bisons wearing stilettos.

Why are things the way they are? Perhaps our hang-ups make things the way they are.

Where do you find peace? In good friendships.

When will you be happy? When I meet a Ryan who isn't a bughead.

How do you know when to stop? When the stop's right in front, with a good friend sitting there waiting for me. And we both buy drinks to watch bisons stamp on bullies, bugheads, and lousy memories.

ABOVE: **Lucas**, acrylic on paper, 2009
OPPOSITE: **Big Hill**, oil pastels and graphite on paper, 2009

216

One of Boe's comin' of age tale.

BY Wong Pixin.

Boe, can we watch cartoons? I'm sick of this game...

Man... just when I'm about done fixing this truck ... okay.

Lemme go grab those tapes from my mom's room.

Cool. What are we watching?

PINK PANTHER!

clank clank

TRUE LOVE

Great! I'll go get us some drinks. You want apple juice? or milk?

Erm. Get me juice, thanks.

Here.. you okay Boe?

I don't know. I just saw my mom... with dad's weener

... in her mouth.

I have no idea what they were doing.

Yeah... I had a friend who saw her parents do that too....

and her mom told her that's what adults do after fight... weird. they It's right?

Yeah it's weird. 'Cause that means mom & Dad don't have to be shouting at each other when they fight.

they can just eat each other weenies and be happy.

OR... maybe they feel stupid for liking that, and they're just making up some excuse...

OH YEAH. That could be it... YUCK!!!

GROSS!!!

End

OPPOSITE: **Boe's Coming-of-Age Tale #2**, ink and graphite on paper, 2010
ABOVE: **Man under Mountain**, crayon and acrylic on paper, 2010

NATE WILLIAMS

Who are you? I am an illustrator originally from the Western United States. I have lived in South and Central America since the end of 2003.

What is your biggest temptation? Skinny waists and big butts.

Why are things the way they are? Luck, choice, and timing.

Where do you find peace? Free time, nature, wife, son, dog, learning, exercise, friends, food, music.

When will you be happy? I dip into the happiness zone on a daily basis.

How do you know when to stop? I don't really stop...something else just captures my interest... I usually return to things...but I like to have a lot of different things going on at the same time.

OPPOSITE: **Melee**, Gooo Calendar, mixed media, 2008
ABOVE: **Horse Dress**, personal work, silkscreen poster,
18 × 24" (46 × 61 cm), 2009

CAITLIN KEEGAN

Who are you? Illustrator, designer, dog owner...triple threat.

What is your biggest temptation? The internet.

Why are things the way they are? How else would they be?

Where do you find peace? On a train, looking out the window.

When will you be happy? See all of the above.

How do you know when to stop? When there's no more space left to fill up.

ABOVE: **Owl Mask**, personal work, pen and ink, digital, 2011
OPPOSITE: **Untitled (Statue)**, personal work, mixed media, 2011

OPPOSITE: **Victorian Moths pattern**, personal work, digital, 2009
ABOVE: **Untitled (Rooster)**, print design for the website
The Working Proof, mixed media, 2011

MIKE PERRY

Who are you? My name is Mike Perry. I have a beard and wear glasses. I am on a journey to discover what happens if I use every art supply in the world. I love color, whisky, black coffee, and puppy dreams.

What is your biggest temptation?
To disappear and live in the woods.

Why are things the way they are?
Because science has made it that way.

Where do you find peace? Peace can be found everywhere, but I usually look under rocks. The heavier, the more peace.

When will you be happy? I currently am.

How do you know when to stop? When it's done. And you may ask how do I know when it's done...I feel it.

ABOVE: **The Circle Made of Other Shapes**, personal work, mixed media, 2011
OPPOSITE: **Joy Box**, Phish, mixed media, 2010

OPPOSITE: **The Town of Ampersand**, personal work, mixed media, 2011
ABOVE LEFT: **I Never Just Wear Socks**, personal work, color pencil, 2011
ABOVE RIGHT: **Shape, Study No. 1**, personal work, mixed media, 2011

ANA BENAROYA

Who are you? I am an introverted observer of the world around me.

What is your biggest temptation? I am tempted by many things, but don't often succumb to them either out of fear or sometimes because of sheer willpower. Sometimes I feel like life is a constant battle against temptation. I feel guilty for giving in and I feel guilty for not giving in... I often wonder what is the right thing to do. Maybe temptation is actually all about guilt.

Why are things the way they are? Because people are creatures of habit and tradition and it's frightening to act or speak differently. The hardest thing in the world is to remain true to yourself and to understand what it is you want in life...and most of the time we don't even know. Because of this people follow paths that have been previously set out by those before them.

Where do you find peace? When walking through the Metropolitan Museum of Art. Despite the overwhelming nature of the museum, I find it very calming to walk through its galleries.

When will you be happy? I will probably never be completely happy. But I also believe true happiness isn't a constant, blissful state of being — it is the acceptance of one's life as it is. I never allow myself to be too content with how things are, at least when it comes to my artwork. I constantly want to improve.

How do you know when to stop? It is something strangely instinctive...like this gut feeling. The tricky thing is to listen to it and not allow your mind to take over. But this is how I approach most of my work, I try to allow things to flow naturally from me rather than over intellectualize. I like analyzing my work after I have created it.

ABOVE: **Sweaty Moustachio**, Carus Publications, gouache on paper, 2011
OPPOSITE: **Cereal Failures**, Mental Floss, ink and digital color, 2012

ABOVE: **Dapper Man**, personal work, gouache on neon paper, 2011
OPPOSITE: **Cotton Club Parade**, Jazz at Lincoln Center, ink and digital color, 2011

Daniel Krall & Jeong Hwa Min on *Mind*

What does mind mean to you?

Daniel Krall: The mind for me is chiefly about processing and storing information, but there have always been discussions about the unused portion and the inner workings that we don't have a really solid grasp of. There's all of this mystical potential locked up in there and a lot of people in recent years have been talking about ideas like collective consciousness and inherited memory/behavior. That sort of thing may or may not be true, but I think it's really interesting. It potentially connects us all to a secret history and helps us to reach back through centuries and touch a part of ourselves that believed in magic and ritual, but slowly found a niche in the modern world. In our desperate search to find something that makes us special and cements our individual identity within billions of other souls that bop around on this Earth with us, all we can do is look inward at our soft grey passenger and hope it's got the information we need to get through all of this.

Jeong Hwa Min: I wanted to connect the themes mind and capitalism together because I think that our society is controlling our minds and that makes us put in the system they created. And we are losing our free mind unconsciously.

Did working with your collaborator change your view on the theme?

DK: Jeong Hwa Min produced these pieces that seemed to deal with confinement, stress, anxiety, memory, and process. Our collaboration was pretty loose, and I'm much more interested in the mind's history and potential. Specifically, memory in a larger sense and its effect on our identity. So, no, not really. I appreciated her specific area of interest within the subject, but I feel like working the way we did allowed for both ideas to communicate separately while working together visually. That way we could cover two distinctly different views of the same subject fairly harmoniously.

JHM: Not so much.

How did you find working together?

DK: From the start, I felt like our work was very different and I thought it would be exciting to try to find a way to make it look good in a shared space. I see what I do as pretty straightforward and narrative. Jeong Hwa Min's work to me is very complex and loaded with symbols and metaphor. While that's not entirely alien to me, I thought it would be much easier to allow her to begin the process in her own visual language and let me react to it after the fact. She produced these great pieces and I just tried to match them in palette and composition.

JHM: At the beginning Daniel suggested creating separate scenes, which are connected, and then a few free-floating characters or objects that can somehow bleed over into the other piece like my old illustration "Kaufhaus". I drew two pages and he figured out how to connect them together for both spreads.

Did you learn something about yourself?

DK: I learned that I like divining meaning and crafting symbols more than I imagined. I always like working with a limited palette, but I especially enjoyed the boldness of the colors she chose, some of which I wouldn't have considered previously. I also learned that I'm much more excited about what we've lost culturally than what we haven't yet achieved.

JHM: It was interesting for me to find out that we could make a story with various illustrations, working with a person whom I have never met and who has a different background.

Will this affect your future work?

DK: I might do more pieces like this, probably within the context of my personal work. It certainly helped me to cut loose a little bit and consider alternative approaches to communicating an idea.

JHM: I want to make four more illustration series with this theme mind. I have already done some about capitalism, education, and war, so I would like to do more about ideology, economy, ageing society, and unequal distributions.

Sophy Hollington & Kyle Platts on *Lost*

What does lost mean to you?

Sophy Hollington: I don't think we intellectualized our theme all that much. I'm a fan of simple and satisfying punchlines in comics, something that's easier to express in more abstract and interesting ways.

Kyle Platts: Well, it's pretty difficult to get lost in this day and age. However, in my first year at university I went clubbing only to black out and wake up in the morning on a bus somewhere on the outskirts of London. That's one of the only times I have been totally lost – it took so long to figure out where I was and get home.

Did working with your collaborator change your view on the theme?

SH: Yeah, I think so. I was going to try and overcomplicate everything and Kyle came up with this great, really simple idea for a comic that I'm really glad we stuck with.

KP: It did change my view on the theme because as we were coming up with ideas for the brief we were forced to think about all the ways in which you can be lost. In our collaboration we created a narrative in which the characters had lost each other.

How did you find working together?

SH: It was a breeze! We both live in London and know each other from university so we met up over milkshakes and worked everything out pretty quickly. We then just cracked on with it really...sending stuff to each other as we finished it so that we could mirror each other's "worlds". I think we'll definitely work together again on a zine or a comic or something.

KP: Because we don't live close to each other we had one initial meeting to discuss ideas, then all of our correspondence was via email. We came up with a format for the piece that made it easy for us to work independently, but we were sharing our progress with each other all the way through the process, which kept the look and feel of our work in sync.

Did you learn something about yourself?

SH: Hmm...I found out I still really love pastels and that working with another person can be insanely rewarding and satisfying. This is my first proper collaboration (that's actually worked) and it's great having someone set a really high standard for you to work to.

KP: I discovered that I really enjoy collaboration. It's something that people should think about doing more often. I think the process of collaboration really helps you develop in your own work, and allows you to achieve things that you wouldn't be able to do on your own.

Will this affect your future work?

SH: Yeah, I think so! I want to do more with others from now on. It's just a matter of finding someone who's easy to work with and whose ideas suit your own.

KP: This has certainly made me want to collaborate again in the future and explore new ideas. I think collaboration is a good learning experience.

Adriana Lozano & Weng Pixin on *Flutter*

ADRIANA LOZANO

Working with Xin was an incredible experience. I really like her work, and exchanging ideas is always good, and even more so when you're having fun doing it. I met Xin in person in 2010 – it was an unexpected meeting which led to a lot of very good things for me. The conversation was easy and personally I'm very happy with the results. When we were given the theme flutter, I told Xin that I'd like to draw bats and she loved the idea. First we looked at some pictures that I had of the Columbian Tairona culture and then we started talking. It's exciting to see that your work can be mixed with someone else's work, as if it were music.

WENG PIXIN

What does flutter mean to you?

Initially, the theme flutter got me thinking about patterns made by inky rorschach tests which often produced pictures that resembled winged creatures. The process of folding the paper and the smearing of ink was something I wanted to try in the collaboration.

Did working with your collaborator change your view on the theme?

Adriana expressed an interest in working on bats. I loved that she picked a somewhat misunderstood creature of flight as a subject for the word flutter which usually conjures prettiness and cuteness. Her works definitely inspired me to work in a more illogical manner to accompany her frenzied lineworks and the strange themes that she often depicts in her art.

How did you find working together?

I really enjoy working with Adriana. She had complete trust in what I do, and I do in her, and that kind of freedom and belief in each other made the whole process really fun.

Did you learn something about yourself?

Well, before we embarked on our collaboration I knew Adriana was gonna be very busy with projects on her side. I like to complete projects way ahead of given deadlines. If someone wants something completed by May, I have it ready by April. So our collaboration has been a learning process to see the good in being much more flexible. After all, she did warn me that she would be busy. I guess, in short: I learnt it is not good to be a control freak when it comes to time and deadlines!

Will this affect your future work?

Yes, I think it has! I am interested to eliminate planning for my current project; to try working in a much more instinctive and improvisational manner.

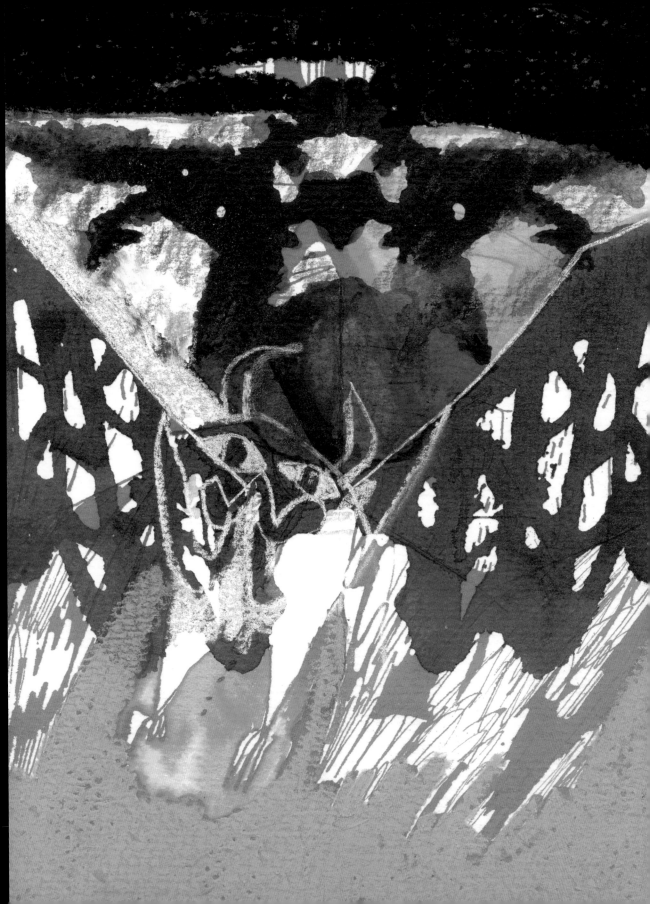

Nate Williams & Caitlin Keegan on *Beast*

What does beast mean to you?

Nate Williams: Beast...hmm...well, I see the idea of a beast as something that you see as having no human qualities and therefore you feel apathy or fear...you dehumanize it so you can treat it badly, guilt free.

Caitlin Keegan: When I was getting started, I looked at a lot of figurines of wild animals from different cultures. I wanted my interpretation of beast to have a primitive and tactile look, so it could almost make sense next to a cave painting or some other early man-made representation.

Did working with your collaborator change your view on the theme?

NW: Not really...I think we collaborated more visually than conceptually.

CK: Nate's artwork introduced an unexpected surreal human element, and I think his creatures seem more invented or imaginary. My beast interpretation leans more into reality even if it isn't totally realistic. Having both depictions interacting within one image definitely adds another layer of meaning.

How did you find working together?

NW: We talked on the phone and then passed files via the internet.

CK: We decided first that we would each start one spread and then switch at the same time. Since both of us like drawing patterns, we agreed that one would be a pattern and the other a full spread image. Nate sent a lot of different pieces that I could incorporate into a repeat pattern, but as I started working on it I was enjoying making it into more of a scene. It was fun to imagine how his different characters could interact with each other and with the new elements that I was introducing. I tried to work the same tiger I had started with into the scene. Having some continuity between the spreads will hopefully create a subtle story when you see the two together.

Did you learn something about yourself?

NW: Yeah, regarding art... I think I like seeing people face to face and brainstorming ideas, but I like to work by myself because art to me is about play and discovery and going down paths without restrictions... When I collaborate with someone I feel I am not as free because, of course, I want to make sure they are happy as well. The great thing about art is you can be a one-man band...whereas I like collaborating on more labor-intensive projects such as animation or web applications because a lot of the time it's too much work for one person, so splitting the work makes sense. However, I must say I like collaborating with my five-year-old son because I love to see how he thinks and making art with him is one of the ways to share that experience.

CK: I think every once in a while it's good to be in a situation where you're not sure what to expect and you have to improvise.

Will this affect your future work?

NW: Yeah, I think I will do more collaborations with kids. I love their logic.

CK: I normally work in Illustrator and by hand with minimal Photoshop, so working mainly in Photoshop layers was a different approach for me, technically. I may try more of this in the future. I think it was good to be out of my comfort zone for a little bit.

Mike Perry & Ana Benaroya on *Iceberg*

What does iceberg mean to you?

Mike Perry: The unknown of what lies beneath.

Ana Benaroya: I didn't start really analyzing and thinking about the theme until I started drawing with Mike. Then I started to think of iceberg as something that is hidden beneath the surface. Something that is suppressed and maybe shameful...or beautiful.

Did working with your collaborator change your view on the theme?

MP: It got crazier.

AB: Not necessarily, although working with him opened me up to a more free way of working...less thinking, more doing. I usually work pretty freely and expressively, but I felt even more like this while working with Mike.

How did you find working together?

MP: It was fun but collaboration is hard. Both people have to be in the right state of mind. They have to constantly trust each other and be willing to make compromises.

AB: It was very pleasant. I went to Mike's studio and we worked together on several sheets of paper for a couple hours, back and forth. It was immediate and quick and we didn't edit anything until afterwards when we digitally altered our drawings and added to them on the computer.

Did you learn something about yourself?

MP: I feel like that's what I am always doing. Sometimes I hate what I learn, sometimes I love what I learn.

AB: That working with another artist is very difficult. I am somewhat of a control freak when it comes to my work. But I'm sure the same can be said of most artists.

Will this affect your future work?

MP: Everything does.

AB: I'm sure. I found working in Mike's studio very inspiring and I love his philosophy of just making stuff, no hesitation.

JEAN-PHILIPPE BRETIN

Who are you? Jean-Philippe Bretin, graphic designer and artist. I also run a magazine about contemporary drawing called *Collection* with some friends.

What is your biggest temptation? The internet. I have some other temptations, but they are not such a waste of time.

Why are things the way they are? Why are things as we think they are? No?

Where do you find peace? I have never felt the sensation of "peace". Maybe I'm not enough of a hippie.

When will you be happy? I am already.

How do you know when to stop? When I feel that to continue would be worse than to stop.

ABOVE LEFT: **Radar**, felt pen, 7 × 10" (17.6 × 25 cm), 2010
ABOVE RIGHT: **Paradoxiah**, felt pen, 7 × 10" (17.6 × 25 cm), 2010
OPPOSITE: **Sacré II**, *Shining* magazine, mixed media, 7 × 10" (17.6 × 25 cm), 2009

OPPOSITE: **Sacré III**, *Shining* magazine, mixed media, 7 × 10" (17.6 × 25 cm), 2009
ABOVE, CLOCKWISE FROM TOP LEFT: **Sans titre (circuit)**, ink on paper, 2009; **Serpan: l'arrestation**, ink on paper, 7 × 10" (17.6 × 25 cm), 2010; **Sans titre (from the zine "Serpan 2")**, ink on paper, 7 × 10" (17.6 × 25 cm), 2011; **Serpan: le bagnard**, ink on paper, 17 × 10" (17.6 × 25 cm), 2010

JEF SCHARF

Who are you? Jef Scharf has been making art with others such as Amy Sillman, Reed Anderson, Elisita Punto, Blok, Mike Smith, Maya Hayuk, and Anna Haifisch since the hippies realized there was a disturbing darkness at the end of their trip. A general lack of confidence in his personal vision led him to adopt the name Wolfy Part II in order to pursue design and musical works. Wolfy owned and operated Kayrock Screen Printing Inc. until he recently sold off his interest. Both identities and his varied pursuits are beginning to come together as one definable artist. Until this occurs he will continue to collaborate with others, including his dual selves.

What is your biggest temptation? "Onion rings and Nancy comics," "chocolate and Jennifer Aniston movies," Helen Keller and plagiarism. At the moment, a Shirley Temple blue glass pitcher and what Rex Reed suggested be done with it.

> "Nothing is ours but our language, our phrasing. If a man takes that from me (knowingly, purposely) he is a thief. If he takes it unconsciously – snaking it out of some old secluded corner of his memory, and mistaking it for a new birth instead of a mummy – he is no thief, and no man has a case against him. Unconscious appropriation is utterly common; it is not plagiarism and is no crime; but conscious appropriation, i. e., plagiarism, is as rare as parricide. Of course there are plagiarists in the world – I am not disputing that – but bless you, they are few and far between. These notions of mine are not guesses; they are the outcome of twenty years of thought and observation upon this subject." – *Mark Twain in a Letter to Robert Burdette, circa April 19, 1890*

Why are things the way they are? "It was a dark and stormy night, we were standing on the deck, the ship was sinking, the captain said to me 'tell me a story my son' and so I began,

It was a dark and stormy night, we were standing on the deck, the ship was sinking, the captain said to me 'tell me a story my son' and so I began. It was a dark and stormy night, we were standing on the deck, the ship was sinking, the captain said to me 'tell me a story my son' and so I began, It was a dark and stormy night, we were standing on the deck, the ship was sinking, the captain said to me 'tell me a story my son' and so I began..." – *Remy Charlip*

Teen hygiene films illustrate that love, rage, and fear are the building blocks of all conflict. Today, I am pretty sure that eventually complete conformity and order or total entropy shall prevail in perpetuity throughout the Universe.

Where do you find peace? I found myself content in the corner of Skyline Books where the Science Fiction section met Hollywood biographies. I continue to be at ease in The Roy and Niuta Titus Theaters and occasionally in The Celeste Bartos Theater.

When will you be happy? A friend who prefers to be cited as a junkie once gave me this advice: "I have known you for some time now and I see you gravitate toward the safety and security of the everyday. The times that you haven't taken the greatest risks are the times that I have seen you happiest and closer than you think to the safety and security that you desire."

How do you know when to stop? You probably should stop when you find yourself on late night television with a bald drummer sporting shades and a scarf, a featherhaired keyboardist, three "session man" guitarists, and a bass player all overacting the intensity of their "jams" while playing your tunes when you damn well know you could still rage on your own. If this doesn't happen then rely on deadlines.

OPPOSITE, CLOCKWISE FROM TOP LEFT: **Taxes, My Race, Your Gun,** "Your Hopes, Your Dreams, My Fears," Street Art, 3-color silkscreen on text-weight paper, Wolfy Part II, except *Taxes* which Anna Haifisch worked on, April 10, 2008; **Sterilize Same Sex Couples,** "Monsters of the Midterm Election," The Scope Foundation, 3-color silkscreen on French brand cover paper, Wolfy Part II, October 2, 2010

TAXES

MY RACE

STERILIZE SAME SEX COUPLES

C.U. Later

YOUR GUN

OPPOSITE: "Glow in the Dark Map of New Jersey," *WFMU*, 3-color silkscreen on French paper, Wolfy Part II with a lot of input from the WFMU staff, 2011
TOP, FROM LEFT TO RIGHT: "Ryonen" book: cover unfolded and inner poster unfolded, personal work, silkscreen on French paper, pictures: Jef Scharf/Wolfy; text: Kid Millions/John Colpitts, September 11, 2012
ABOVE "The Sixth Annual Brahloween feat: famous movie actors out of makeup," *Oneida*, silkscreen on black cover-weight paper, Wolfy Part II, 2010

ORIT BERGMAN

Who are you? An illustrator, a writer of children's books and plays, a mom to two kids, one dog(ette), a three-legged cat, five chickens, and an unknown number of goldfish.

What is your biggest temptation? Smart people, shoes, new translations of classic Russian books, and good food.

Why are things the way they are? I wish I believed things are the way they are because there is a big plan, one which I don't understand. Unfortunately, I believe things are the way they are because a yellow dog just crossed the road, as much as they are influenced by my actions and wishes. Still I act as if my actions and wishes are more important than the yellow dog crossing the street.

Where do you find peace? I find peace when I swim at sea, especially when it starts getting cold outside in November, but the water is still warm. I find it when I get up early, before the whole family, and I have some time to myself, and, finally, when I color while Skyping with my best friend.

When will you be happy? I hope today. Happiness is kind of tricky, when you're happy you think it will last forever, and when you're not it seems like it will never come. And even though I know this for a fact, that it comes and goes, I have little control over it. One thing for sure is that I'm always happy when a children's book of mine is published.

How do you know when to stop? I don't. Sometimes it's an advantage, especially with long projects. I think I do my best work when I have a long time and a body of work to do, like when I create sets and illustrations for the theatre, a book, or illustrations for a children's museum. I then have time to find the right language and to develop it over time. With shorter projects I usually stop at the deadline, but a sure way to know that I overdid it is when I start hating the work. Luckily, I work on the computer so I can revert to an earlier version. Undo is one of my favorite actions; I wish someone would come up with a way to implement it outside the computer.

ABOVE: Unpublished piece made as a sketch for a children's exhibition on the subject of the Hebrew language
OPPOSITE: Poster (one in a series) for a performance called "K" at the Clipa Theater at the Jersalem Festival, 2010

OPPOSITE: Poster (one in a series) for a performance called "K" at the
Clipa Theater at the Jersalem Festival 2010
ABOVE: **Night Run**, self promotion, pencil and computer work, 2011

267

YOSUKE YAMAGUCHI

Who are you? I am Yosuke Yamaguchi. I was born and am now residing in Tokyo, Japan. I began my career as a designer and eventually started painting and studied at Setsu Mode Seminar. I am now working as a painter and designer. I have had painting exhibitions at a contemporary art gallery and also completed illustrations for Japanese magazines such as *Soen*, *ecocolo*, *In the City* (by Beams Cultuart), and magazines abroad such as *Plant Journal* (Spain), *Frédéric Magazine* (France), and for musicians such as Yann Tomita, Hauschka, Mantler, and beautiful Hummingbird. I recently sold a reprint of one of my painting at 20 × 200 organized by Jen Bekman which is a gallery in New York.

What is your biggest temptation? Watching YouTube or sleeping.

Why are things the way they are? I think there's no reason for it. There's some secret· structure or some kind of theory which is basically hidden from people and sometimes you're able to, or maybe allowed to, take a glance at it by creating things or doing whatever is appropriate for each person. It doesn't have to be "Art". It could be anything — baking a pie, riding a bicycle, walking a dog, but there's this certain moment when you get connected to this feeling that exceeds people's general knowledge. But there isn't any single reason for it. It just exists and there's nothing we can do about it.

Where do you find peace? When I get connected to that certain moment and feel the tip of the secret enormous unknown structure of the world as I said in the question above.

When will you be happy? Same answer as to Q.2 and 4.

How do you know when to stop? Same answer as to Q.4. I get excited from my heart and I just know it. It may take time to reach that point but once you know it, you know it. It happens in a moment.

ABOVE: **Slow Ending**, gesso, watercolor, and acrylic on wood panel, print on 20 x 200, 2010
OPPOSITE: **Someday**, gesso, watercolor, and acrylic print on 20 x 200, 2011

OPPOSITE: **Queen of Europe**, acrylic, watercolor, and gesso, 2010
ABOVE: **We Will Meet**, gesso, watercolor, and acrylic on paper, 2010

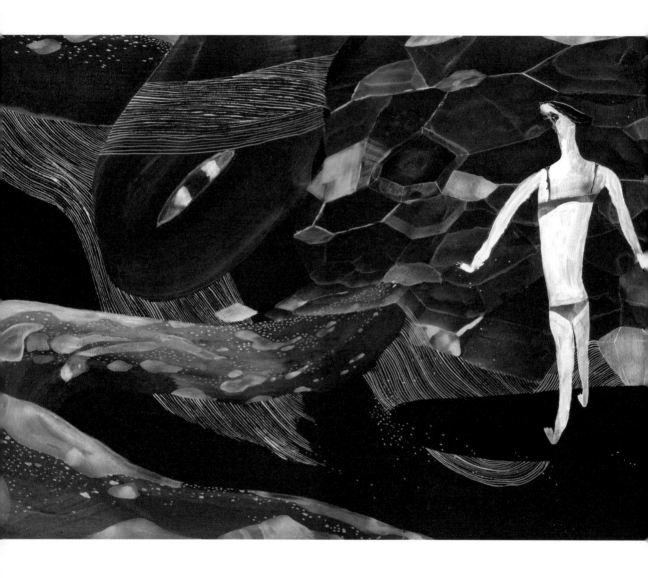

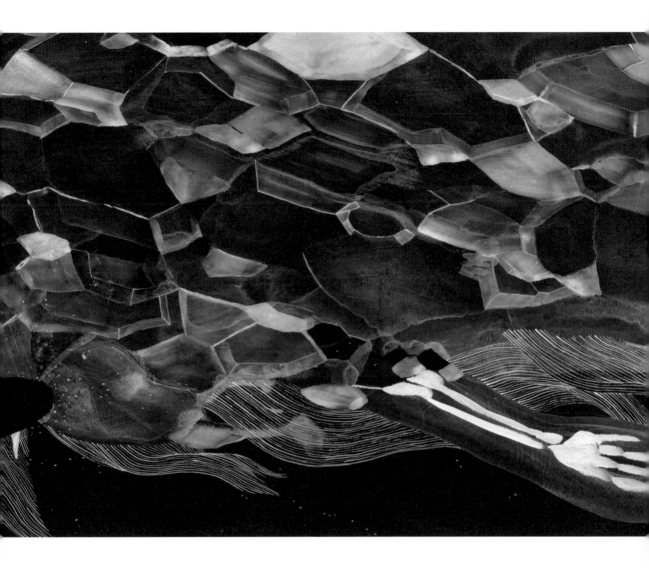

Sufer Girl, personal work,
gesso, watercolor, and acrylic on cardboard, 2011

JULIA
ROTHMAN

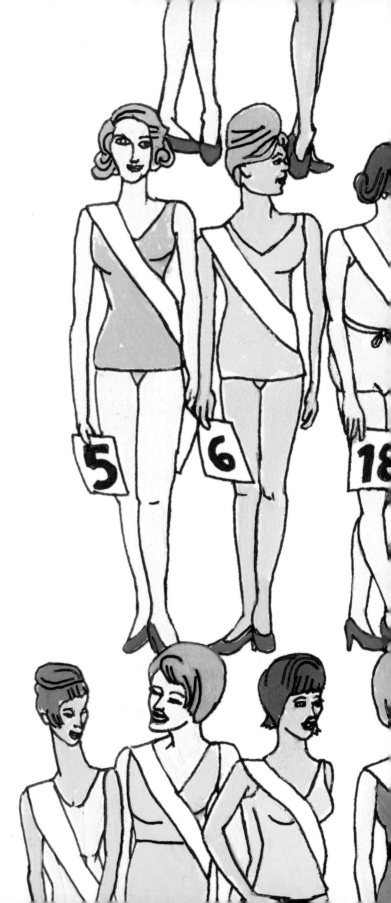

Who are you? I am tall and wear size 11 shoes.
I love what I do for a living. I have always lived
in New York City and probably always will.

What is your biggest temptation? To quit
doing art and become a dancer.

Why are things the way they are? Because
I haven't had time to fix them.

Where do you find peace? In my bed, when
I am warm and under the covers before
falling asleep. I look forward to that moment
every day.

When will you be happy? I probably won't.
I am forever looking for the next thing before
the last one finishes. I am never satisfied
with myself or my work or my personal life.
There is always more to do and ways to make
things better.

How do you know when to stop? You don't
ever stop, that means giving up.

Beauty Queens, personal work,
gouache and ink, 2009

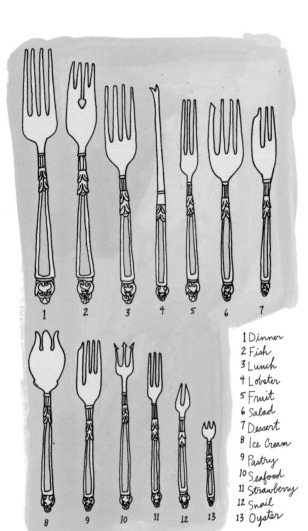

1 Dinner
2 Fish
3 Lunch
4 Lobster
5 Fruit
6 Salad
7 Dessert
8 Ice Cream
9 Pastry
10 Seafood
11 Strawberry
12 Snail
13 Oyster

ABOVE LEFT: **Forks**, Design Sponge, 2009
ABOVE RIGHT: **Ironstone**, Design Sponge, 2009
OPPOSITE: **Adventure Poster**, MTA Arts for Transit, 2010

Verrazano-Narrows Bridge

The Brooklyn Museum

Statue of Liberty

Jean Shin's Celadon Remnants

Rockefeller Center

Flatiron building

Sol LeWitt's Whirls and twirls (MTA)

South Street Seaport

Bronx Zoo

Chrysler Building

Bryant Park

Guggenheim Museum

Vito Acconci's Wall-Slide

Roy Lichtenstein's Times Square Mural

Van Siclen Av

Barbara Ellmann's The View From Here

GRAND CENTRAL TERMINAL

Grand Central Terminal

Hudson River Trail

Jane Greengold and Kana Chand Do Almost Home

American Museum of Natural History

TRU KNOWLEDGE VISA

Union Square Farmers Market

Subway N Q R W S T E F 6

Empire State Building

SUBWAY

Yumi Heo's Q is for Queens

Brooklyn Bridge

277

AMY BROWN

Who are you? If I were writing my GCSE German exam I'd say "Hallo, mein Name ist Amy Brown. Ich habe braune Haare und braune Augen. Ich mag Kunst." However, I failed my German GCSE exam so that's as far as it would go. Answering now I'd say I've reached an age where I know with absolute surety that my inner core will not change. I'm pleased with this as it's a good one. The other parts of myself that include habits, lovely bits, and flaws get tweaked hopefully just often enough to adapt successfully to my surroundings and to make friends. As far as the future Amy Brown... Well, I'm really looking forward to finding out about her.

What is your biggest temptation? I want to say pizza, beer, and *Back to the Future*, but in truth it's those pesky antique bargains that get me every time! I could quite easily get lost for hours in the mayhem of flea markets and boot fairs. Sometimes the stall owners are just as fascinating as the wonderful objects they're selling.

Why are things the way they are? Err, with the world or with me? Hmm, if me, then I guess it's because I think mainly in pictures.

Visual stimulation is my life, it's what gets me unbelievably excited about being alive. The idea of being able to make a living from work I adore creating is something I will never take for granted. It's not been easy. You definitely get used to living on a budget! But I wouldn't swap it and I guess that's why I'm still drawing. With the world? Hmm, we probably need some more of those rooms where dinosaurs, kittens, and unicorns can just get along.

When will you be happy? Wow, maybe never. Actually, I'm genuinely really easily pleased by the smallest of things and pretty optimistic but I guess like a lot of creatives I have down days, but by frequently doing all of the bits mentioned in question three I stay pretty darn positive and happy. In the grand scheme of things, to write and illustrate children's books that inspire children and resonate throughout their adulthood, THAT would make me happy. That would be unbelievably awesome.

How do you know when to stop? When your eyes start to bleed and you get the shakes.

ABOVE: **Chillaxing**, personal work, for a mini book called *BBQs are Hot*, acrylic, 2011
OPPOSITE: **Boiled Shrooms**, personal work, acrylic

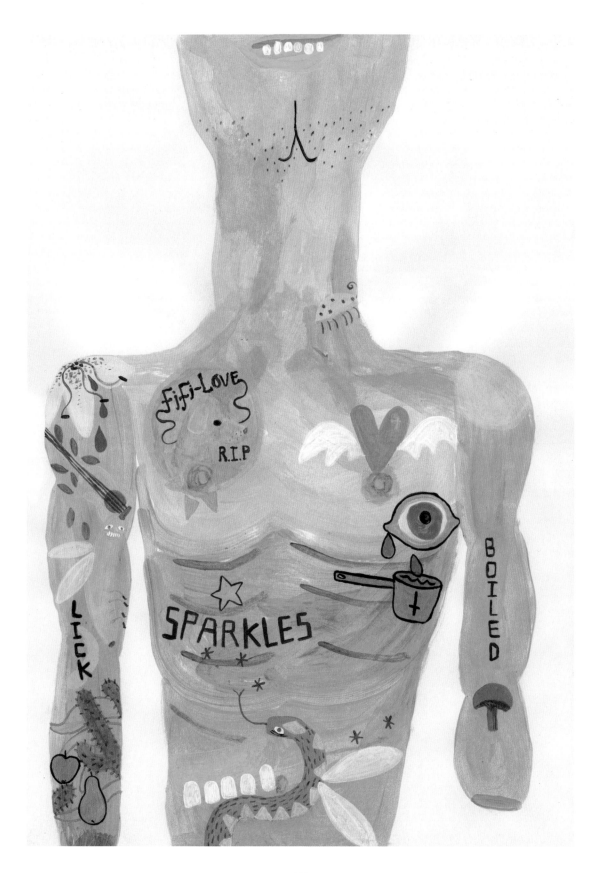

ABOVE: From a book called *Monster Max*, personal work, acrylic
OPPOSITE: From a pitch for a Casio watchstrap, acrylic

NIV BAVARSKY

Who are you? My name is Niv Bavarsky. I've only met one other Niv in my life, although I hear there are a bunch of others. I think I'm named after another Niv, but I don't know anything about him. The Niv I met was a 10-year-old boy who told me he knows more about cartoons than I do and has seen more beards than I've seen. I tried arguing with him, because I am very stubborn, but then my mom made fun of me for debating with a 10-year-old. She was right.

What is your biggest temptation? Apathy and inaction—like a lot of my generation, I guess. It can be difficult to summon the motivation to overcome inertia. It's a little too easy to tune out the world, I think.

Why are things the way they are? Sometimes I imagine time and circumstance as this enormous ring of dominoes, stretching out infinitely (or, at least, extremely far, further than is reasonable to take the time to imagine)—one enormous and constant chain reaction, so large you can hardly see any of it all. I don't know why things are the way they are.

Where do you find peace? In moments. It's almost completely unpredictable, though, sometimes drawing is the most peaceful thing in the world, sometimes it makes me want to pull out my hair. I can definitely say, though, that my most sublime and peaceful moments have come during the act of creating something. I often feel slightly out of step with the world, but not when I'm making stuff.

When will you be happy? I don't know. At various points along the way. Hopefully at the end, too.

How do you know when to stop? I often don't. Sometimes, though, you just know.

ABOVE: **Cowboy Drawing**, personal work, ink on paper, 9 × 12" (23 × 30 cm), 2009
OPPOSITE: **Wedding**, personal work, gouache on paper, 10 × 13" (25 × 33 cm), 2012

SOMEPLACE FLAT,
AND EMPTY.

ABOVE: **Someplace Flat and Empty**, personal work, gouache on paper, 2010
OPPOSITE: **Deadzone**, personal work, gouache and ink on Bristol, 19 × 24"
(48 × 61 cm)

SAM VANALLEMEERSCH

A STAR IS BORN

Who are you? I'm a Belgian person who likes to draw things.

What is your biggest temptation? Cigarettes.

Why are things the way they are? This question eats itself like an Ouroboros.

Where do you find peace? Concrete spaces and bed-time readings of sci-fi books.

When will you be happy? The (flawed) concept of happiness doesn't interest me.

How do you know when to stop? Just enough black, just enough white. But then I just start over again.

ABOVE: **Mothra sketchbook**, ink, 2012
OPPOSITE: **I believe we might have… a problem**, personal work, ink and gouache, 2012

ABOVE: **Upload Downtown Movie Festival Poster**, ink, 2012
OPPOSITE: **Strip Turnhout**, magazine cover, ink and ecoline, digital, 2012

SHIGEKO OKADA

Who are you? I was born and grew up in the suburbs of Tokyo. After working in the financial field, I shifted gear to pursue my ultimate dream of becoming an illustrator in New York. I may look like a serious and quiet person, on first impression, but I am always secretly looking for funny moments in my daily life. And, I do love cats.

What is your biggest temptation? The two worlds of vintage and antique.

Why are things the way they are? I believe that things all concern Karma. Looking back on my life, I realized that some events happened for no reason. If I think like this then I can accept things easily when I encounter difficulties in my life.

Where do you find peace? At home with my beloved cat. Even if she comes in contact with me in an unfriendly manner at the end of the day I feel peace.

When will you be happy? Having dinner at home with good friends. I like to invite my close friends for dinner and have a good conversation over a glass of wine and to be invited for dinner by my friends as well.

How do you know when to stop? When I've lost my concentration. Usually, I can concentrate on what I am doing for quite a long time.

ABOVE: **Oregon Map**, personal work, gouache, 2011
OPPOSITE: **Portrait of Truck Driver**, portrait commission, gouache , 2011

292

OPPOSITE: **Weekend**, personal work, gouache, 2012
ABOVE: **MJ and B**, personal work, gouache, 2011

KEIKO TOKUSHIMA

Who are you? I am an illustrator who is currently working in New York City. I was born and raised in Hiroshima, Japan.

What is your biggest temptation? My biggest temptation is that I want to see things which I'm not allowed to see.

Why are things the way they are? Because the socially dominant groups define the way they are.

Where do you find peace? I find peace when I get close to nature because my hometown is surrounded by mountains and sea. Nature is also one of my biggest inspirations.

When will you be happy? I think when I make people happy.

How do you know when to stop? When I feel confident and satisfied with a thing that has to be done.

ABOVE LEFT: **Cosmic World**, personal work, acrylic on paper, 2010
ABOVE RIGHT: **The Kitchen**, personal work, acrylic on paper, 2010
OPPOSITE: **Early Summer**, personal work, acrylic on paper, 2010

ABOVE LEFT: **Rod Serling**, personal work, acrylic on paper, 2010
ABOVE RIGHT: **The Most Unusual Camera**, personal work, acrylic on paper, 2010
OPPOSITE: **Woody Allen**, *NY Japion*, acrylic on paper, 2011

Jean-Philippe Bretin & Jef Scharf on *Melting*

What does melting mean to you?

Jean-Philippe Bretin: I saw the theme of melting as more like an instruction, a way to approach the illustration. That allowed us to start collaborating with this aim in mind, then things evolved...

Jef Scharf: I have never really thought about melting all that much, maybe once a season or over a frying pan.

Did working with your collaborator change your view on the theme?

J-PB: The theme is pretty broad, so I never really had a fixed idea of it. We focused on coming up with good images, rather than sticking rigidly to the theme. Working as a pair implies a kind of fusion, anyway; our files were merged together on computers that were thousands of miles apart. That's a sort of melting, isn't it?

JS: Yes, Jean-Philippe pointed out that rather than things melting, we were supposed to melt visually together in the collaboration. It got me thinking about different forms and meanings of the theme – places where melting had meaning. I remembered a story about an icicle being used as a murder weapon in *Two-Minute Mysteries* by Donald J. Sobol.

How did you find working together?

J-PB: Working with someone you don't know is pretty amazing. Even with my illustrator friends, we rarely collaborate; it's fun but I'm rarely convinced by the results. With Jef, we exchanged emails, he sent me lots of starting points for pieces, separate elements, some really good stuff. I tried to continue those drawings, adding elements, which didn't always work. I sent him the ones I liked best, and we kept working on the chosen image. Eventually, we selected an image from the ones we'd produced.

JS: It was difficult because of the physical distance and specific changes happening in our lives both personally and professionally. The exchanges happened over electronic media instead of the postal system which I had hoped to employ. The aspect of physically handling and manipulating something adds to the patina that develops in the collaborative process.

Did you learn something about yourself?

J-PB: Ha, I don't think so. I haven't really thought about it.

JS: I am lazy and I often miss details of things that hover solely on computer screens. I often wait for the foundation to build upon in the collaborative process instead of creating it.

Will this affect your future work?

J-PB: Actually, it had been a while since I did any illustration; I've been doing a lot of graphic design lately. This has really made me want to do some new stuff.

JS: Yes, almost everything does except Alfred Kubin. I suppose that if I consciously don't allow something to affect my work then, in fact, it does.

<u>Orit Bergman &</u>
<u>Yosuke Yamaguchi</u> on *<u>Born</u>*

<u>What does born mean to you?</u>

Orit Bergman: We decided to make one illustration by ourselves and the second as a collaboration. The first piece I did was more personal. As a twin, I always felt birth was the minute of separation not only from my mother but also from my twin sister. Although our lives have taken different paths, I feel that they are still strongly connected.

Yosuke Yamaguchi: Maybe it's all about circulation. We didn't just come from nowhere. I kind of feel the life before I was formed as I am right now and I want to feel that through what I do.

<u>Did working with your collaborator change your view on the theme?</u>

OB: When I worked with Yos I was interested more in birth as part of the cycle of life and death, everything that is born will die, and so the moment of birth holds the minute of death. The image of the baby boy riding the skeleton of a rabbit came right to my mind and I started from there. I love the contrast between our notion of a baby with a bunny and the image.

YY: Yes, Orit is a twin and she sent me the picture of her and her sister when they were kids. She said she couldn't tell which one is her. This was very interesting and made me think about how you keep your own identity.

<u>How did you find working together?</u>

OB: Illustration doesn't offer many occasions for collaborating and this is one of the few things I don't like about my job, so I was very excited about the project. I had lots of fun working with Yos, his technique and his ideas are very different from mine – he brought to the image stories from Japanese culture, a sense of mystery and terrific colors. I never use purple in my work, it's the hardest color to work with, but after this collaboration I have added it to my palette. We worked in turn, each time adding in whatever we felt like and sending the work to the other side of the world. Some stuff was thrown away during the process but most was left in. Waiting to see what Yos would send back was the most fun part of this work.

YY: We exchanged Photoshop files, taking turns, and added our drawings one by one. It was very exciting to see the new piece and how the picture had changed and progressed beyond what we had intended. We decided on the basic way to do the collaboration and after that we didn't need to talk much about what we did. I think we had similar taste in what we like.

<u>Did you learn something about yourself?</u>

OB: (no response)

YY: Not really. As usual.

<u>Will this affect your future work?</u>

OB: Usually, I can see the effects of a work a long time after it's finished, so hopefully the answer to this question will change with time. It's like launching paper boats on a lake: you never know when you will bump into one in the future.

YY: This was the first time I have collaborated out of the country and it was very interesting. It will surely affect my future work.

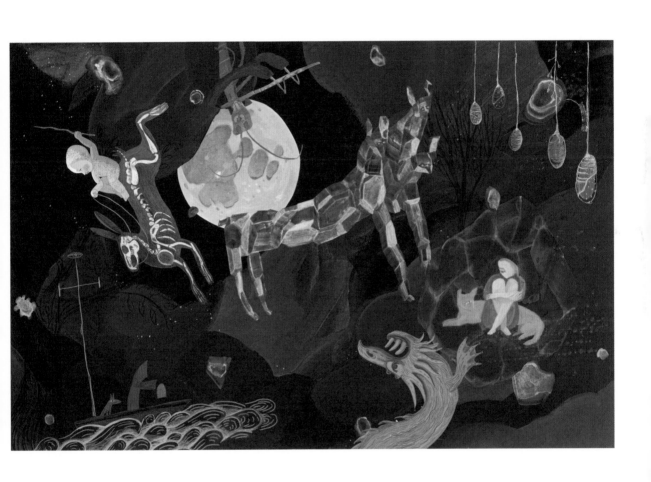

Julia Rothman & Amy Brown on *Fight*

What does fight mean to you?

Julia Rothman: When we got the theme fight I immediately imagined a battle of some kind. The word fight brings up feelings of struggle and intensity. Fighting is what happens when you disagree or clash so it definitely has negative connotations.

Amy Brown: We had the theme fight so automatically it conjured up images of our different styles fighting for attention on the page. It made sense to go with this and let our characters do battle.

Did working with your collaborator change your view on the theme?

JR: We were able to have a lot of fun in "our fight" because Amy's work is so playful. Her colorful characters brought humor to our piece and the fight became a lot less serious.

AB: Luckily, we were both keen to have some fun and be pretty obvious with it – we both just wanted to see carnage! So I guess no, it didn't change my view, but only because we agreed from the start.

How did you find working together?

JR: It was great working with Amy! She lives so far away but we communicated perfectly via email. When we got the theme I immediately had the idea of each of us doing a facing page with our characters prepared for a battle and then collaborating on the aftermath of the war. Amy was up for anything and did such an awesome job creating her scene. Then I pulled some of her color palette and made my side. I was the slacker of the two of us and she was able to push me along to get our second piece finally finished. I wound up sending her all my beaten up people and horses and she put the final composition for the spread together. When she sent me the image to see what I thought, I laughed out loud. I love how she set it all up, especially my guy throwing up over her donut man.

AB: Julia came across as a lovely person, really up for getting excited about the work. I'd seen her art before so I was really excited to be partnered with her, if not a little

nervous. The project was actually amazingly uncomplicated with regards to deciding what we were doing. We knew we had four pages in total so we decided to have a page each to show off our own armies and then have them mixed up and interacting on the double spread. We took it in turns to email our single pages over to each other so that we could line up our backgrounds. For the double page I sent Julia my beaten up characters and then she sent me a page of hers so that I could compile them together. Thankfully we agreed on the layout straightaway and after a double thumbs up it was ready. I think throughout the entire process we had a few "how's it going" kind of emails but the actual work part was confined to not many at all.

Did you learn something about yourself?

JR: I'm usually the leader in a group and I like to have full control. But I quickly let go of that when I was working with Amy because I knew she would do a great job. And when I asked her if she would arrange the second spread, I was so pleased with what she did. I couldn't have done a better job so I'm so glad I stepped down from that role. It might be something I try more often.

AB: I've learnt that I really enjoy making simple narratives, it's been really good practice for future story books. I've also learnt that you should always paint all versions of one character at the same time! I was silly and did some on separate days... Apparently, I used a really elusive combination of colors for some of them.

Will this affect your future work?

JR: I do a lot of collaborative work and hope to continue doing more. I think it makes you try things you never otherwise would. I really like the colors I used in my piece and those never would have come together without Amy's influence.

AB: It's made me open to collaboration projects for sure. It would depend on who they were with but it's made me realize it can be a wonderfully uncomplicated process and that the result can potentially be far more creative than a solo one.

Niv Bavarsky &
Sam Vanallemeersch
on *Fire*

What does fire mean to you?

Niv Bavarsky: Fire destroys things, but it also helps to create them, and it can be very pretty if it isn't burning down your home. It feels good on your eyes.

Sam Vanallemeersch: To me it sounds a bit too much like a typical theme. A theme or subject such as "the geopolitical evolution in the farming industry of southern Mesopotamia in 2000 BC" would've been more appropriate, I think, as it narrows it down, but, on the other hand, opens up a lot of possibilities. I'll be honest: I'm not into themes in general.

Did working with your collaborator change your view on the theme?

NB: Working with a collaborator always sets you on a direction you didn't initially expect, which is the best part about it. Fire became a character trait to build narratives around.

SV: Partially.

How did you find working together?

NB: We live on different continents, so we worked in phases, trading files via the internet. This was the first time I've collaborated with a visual artist over the internet in this fashion. Honestly, we kept discussion very brief for the most part, and let the drawings speak for themselves.

SV: Waiting for an email, drawing, sending an email once again, watching a movie, drawing, and so forth. Not a lot of conversations though.

Did you learn something about yourself?

NB: I think so. I have been doing a lot of collaborative drawings recently, in person, with artists who live near me, but this makes me much more interested in pursuing collaborations with more international artists in the future. The internet is very powerful.

SV: Collaboration, together with themes, are not my forte. So all this stuff made me nervous. I sort of already knew this, but decided to give it a go.

Will this affect your future work?

NB: Doesn't everything?

SV: Nope. But coffee will.

Shigeko Okada & Keiko Tokushima on *Prayer*

What does prayer mean to you?

Shigeko Okada: My theme is prayer and the 3.11 earthquake disaster in Japan crossed my mind. Then, coexisting with nature became the theme of this project.

Keiko Tokushima: My theme prayer signifies one of the methods to show my gratitude and respect for nature. This is the reason why my collaborator and I decided to represent prayer through nature.

Did working with your collaborator change your view on the theme?

SO: Not really. We have almost the same point of view on the theme.

KT: Not very much. We both have the same opinions and thoughts on this theme. However, Shigeko brought some different perspectives to it through our discussions and that encouraged me to gain deeper thoughts on it.

How did you find working together?

SO: The most difficult part is the time difference and the distance between Tokyo and New York. After talking about the theme over and over and how to collaborate via Skype, we decided to collaborate as much as we could: one person sketched and painted the foreground and another did the background, one person sketched and another painted it.

KT: Shigeko and I have been close friends since we attended the same school with majors in illustration. We had dual shows a couple times, but have never done collaborative

work together before. I always love her work and thought that collaborating with each other would enrich our experiences as artists. As we discussed how we'd like to describe prayer with illustrations, both of us agreed that we didn't want to go to the theme with clichés, such as a person praying for something. We came up with the idea of "nature worship" after research and brainstorming. Nowadays, it is so easy to forget that we receive the blessings of nature everyday because most things we need from nature are easy to obtain regardless of regions, seasons, and so forth. And that makes the processes of nature even harder to see. Especially now as appreciation and respect for nature are fashionable, we need to redefine the relationship between humans and nature. We hope that our work will be a trigger for more talks about this.

Did you learn something about yourself?

SO: I realized that I have my own color scheme. I chose a color I don't usually use so that it fitted the image by my partner.

KT: Yes, I learned about my feelings towards nature.

Will this affect your future work?

SO: I believe so. This unique opportunity gave me a new view on illustration, and I really enjoyed creating works with Ms. Keiko Tokushima.

KT: Yes, it will. I have learned that our society is disconnected from nature. We have chosen to walk away from it both spiritually and physically.

I would like to reflect that in my future work.

First and foremost, I want to thank all the artists who agreed to participate in this book. The amount of effort they put into the collaborations and the interviews was huge. I cannot thank them enough.

I would also like to thank Thames & Hudson for being interested in my book idea and for wanting to publish my first book. I am extremely honored.

And, finally, I would like to thank my parents for always supporting my interest in art and for never doubting me.

Ana Albero
www.ana-albero.com

Gerard Armengol
www.gerardarmengol.com

Jordan Awan
www.jordanawan.com

Niv Bavarsky
www.nivbavarsky.com

Drew Beckmeyer
www.drewbeckmeyer.com

Ana Benaroya
www.anabenaroya.com

Orit Bergman
www.oritbergman.com

Paul Blow
www.paulblow.com

Jean-Philippe Bretin
www.jeanphilippebretin.com

Amy Brown
www.amyillustration.com

Café con Leche
Inés: www.inechi.com
Roi: www.roibotapache.tumblr.com

Ryan Cecil Smith
www.ryancecilsmith.com

Henrik Drescher
www.hdrescher.com

Gustavo Eandi
www.gustavoeandi.com

Ekta
www.ekta.nu

Jan Feliks Kallwejt
www.kallwejt.com

Sophy Hollington
www.sophyhollington.com

Jeong Hwa Min
www.sugarlandparadise.com

James Jirat Patradoon
www.jiratpatradoon.com

Caitlin Keegan
www.caitlinkeegan.com

Marina Kharkover
www.marinakharkover.com

Daniel Krall
www.danielkrall.com

Paul Loubet
www.gregoletpoluar.com/poluar

Adriana Lozano
www. adrianalozanoroman.blogspot.com.ar
www.flickr.com/photos/adriana_lozano_r

Benjamin Marra
www.benjaminmarra.com

Yu Matsuoka
www.yumatsuokapol.com

Shigeko Okada
www.shigeko-okada.com

Paul Paetzel
www.flickr.com/photos/15680350@N05

Mu Pan
www.mupan.com

Mike Perry
www.mikeperrystudio.com

Weng Pixin
www.rollinghometoyou.blogspot.com

Kyle Platts
www.kyleplatts.com

Josephin Ritschel
www.mevameva.de

Edel Rodriguez
www.edelr.com

Jungyeon Roh
www.jungyeonroh.com

Julia Rothman
www.juliarothman.com

Simon Roussin
www.simon-roussin.com

Jef Scharf (from Kayrock)
www.wolfypartii.blogspot.com

Whitney Sherman
www.whitneysherman.com

Yuko Shimizu
www.yukoart.com

Shoboshobo
www.shoboshobo.com

Ahu Sulker
www.ahusulker.com

Keiko Tokushima
www.keikotokushima.com

Sam Vanallemeersch
www.kolchoz.com

Brecht Vandenbroucke
www.brechtvandenbroucke.blogspot.com

Nate Williams
www.n8w.com/gallery/tags/images

Yosuke Yamaguchi
www.blogs.dion.ne.jp/bonfire

Olimpia Zagnoli
www.olimpiazagnoli.com

Irkus M. Zeberio
www.irkus.net

Zeloot
www.zeloot.nl

Ana Benaroya is an illustrator based in Jersey City, USA. Her
work has been honoured by the Society of Illustrators, American
Illustration and the PRINT Regional Design Annual. Among her
clients are the Lincoln Center, *The New Yorker*, *The New York Times*,
Marc Ecko, WILCO, and ABC World News Tonight.

Front cover: Ekta
Back cover: Ana Albero

Illustration Next © 2013 Ana Benaroya

Individual illustrations © 2013 the artists

Designed by Therese Vandling

First published in 2013 in hardcover in the United States of America
by Thames & Hudson Inc., 500 Fifth Avenue, New York, New York 10110

thamesandhudsonusa.com

Library of Congress Catalog Card Number 2012956284

ISBN 978-0-500-51701-7

Printed and bound in China by C & C Offset Printing Co. Ltd.